MW01265543

THE
LAW OF
SUCCESS

LESSONS TEN AND ELEVEN

Teaching, for the First Time in the History of the World, the True
Philosophy upon which all Personal Success is Built.

BY

NAPOLEON HILL

Originally published by The RALSTON UNIVERSITY PRESS
MERIDEN, CONN.

© **Copyright 2006 – BN Publishing**

www.bnpublishing.com

Printed in the U.S.A.

Lesson Ten

PLEASING PERSONALITY

"You Can Do It if You Believe You Can!"

WHAT is an ATTRACTIVE personality?

Of course the answer is: A personality that attracts.

But what causes a personality to attract? Let us proceed to find out. Your personality is the sum total of your characteristics and appearances which distinguish you from all others. The clothes you wear, the lines in your face, the tone of your voice, the thoughts you think, the character you have developed by those thoughts - all constitute parts of your personality.

Whether your personality is attractive or not is another matter.

By far the most important part of your personality is that which is represented by your character, and is therefore the part that is not visible. The style of your clothes and their appropriateness undoubtedly constitute a very important part of your personality, for it is true that people form first impressions of you from your outward appearance.

Even the manner in which you shake hands forms an important part of your personality, and goes a very long way toward attracting or repelling those with whom you shake hands.

This art can be cultivated.

The expression of your eyes also forms an important part of your personality, for there are people, and they are more numerous than one might imagine, who can look through your eyes into your heart and see that which is written there by the nature of your most secret thoughts.

The vitality of your body - sometimes called personal magnetism - also constitutes an important part of your personality.

Now let us proceed to arrange these outward mediums through which the nature of our personality is expressed, so that it will attract and not repel.

There is one way in which you can so express the composite of your personality that it will always attract, even though you may be as homely as the circus "fat woman," and this is by -

5

Taking a keen heart-interest in the other fellow's "game" in life.

Let me illustrate exactly what is meant, by relating an incident that happened some years ago, from which I was taught a lesson in master salesmanship.

One day an old lady called at my office and sent in her card with a message saying that she must see me personally. No amount of coaxing by secretaries could induce her to disclose the nature of her visit, therefore I made up my mind that she was some poor old soul who wanted to sell me a book, and remembering that my own mother was a woman, I decided to go out to the reception room and buy her book, whatever it might be.

Please follow every detail thoughtfully, for you, too, may learn a lesson in master salesmanship from this incident.

As I walked down the hallway from my private office, this old lady, who was standing just outside of the railing that led to the main reception room, began to smile.

I had seen many people smile, but never before had I seen one who smiled so sweetly as did this lady. It was one of those contagious smiles, because I caught the spirit of it and began to smile also.

As I reached the railing the old lady extended her hand to shake hands with me. Now, as a rule, I do not become too friendly on first acquaintance when a person calls at my office, for the reason that it is very hard to say "no" if the caller should ask me to do that which I do not wish to do.

However, this dear old lady looked so sweetly innocent and harmless that I extended my hand and she began to shake it! Whereupon, I discovered that she not only had an attractive smile, but she also had a magnetic handshake. She took hold of my hand firmly, but not too firmly, and the very manner in which she went about it telegraphed the thought to my brain that it was she who was doing the honors. She made me feel that she was really and truly glad to shake my hand, and I believe that she was. I believe that her handshake came from the heart as well as from the hand.

I have shaken hands with many thousands of people during my public career, but I do not recall having ever done so with anyone who understood the art of doing it as well as this old lady did. The moment she touched my hand I could feel myself "slipping," and I knew that whatever it was that she had come after she would go away with it, and that I would aid and abet her all I could toward this end.

In other words, that penetrating smile and that warm hand-shake had disarmed me and made me a "willing victim." At a single stroke this old lady had shorn me of that false shell into which I crawl when salesmen come around selling or trying to sell that which I do not want. To go back to an expression which you found quite frequently in previous lessons of this course, this gentle visitor had "neutralized" my mind and made me want to listen.

Ah, but here is the stumbling point at which most salespeople fall and break their necks, figuratively speaking, for it is as useless to try to sell a man something until you have first made him want to listen, as it would be to command the earth to stop rotating.

Note well how this old lady used a smile and a handshake as the tools with which to pry open the window that led to my heart; but the most important part of the transaction is yet to be related.

Slowly and deliberately, as if she had all the time there was in the universe (which she did have, as far as I was concerned at that moment) the old lady began to crystallize the first step of her victory into reality by saying:

"I just came here to tell you (what seemed to me to be a long pause) that I think you are doing the most wonderful work of any man in the world today."

Every word was emphasized by a gentle, though firm squeeze of my hand, and she was looking through my eyes and into my heart as she spoke.

After I regained consciousness (for it became a standing joke among my assistants at the office that I fainted dead away), I reached down and unlocked the little secret latch that fastened the gate and said:

"Come right in, dear lady - come right into my private office," and with a gallant bow that would have done credit to the cavaliers of olden times, I bade her come in and "sit awhile."

As she entered my private office, I motioned her to the big easy-chair back of my desk while I took the little hard-seated chair which, under ordinary circumstances, I would have used as a means of discouraging her from taking up too much of my time.

For three-quarters of an hour I listened to one of the most brilliant and charming conversations I have ever heard, and my visitor was doing all of the conversing. From the very start she had assumed the initiative and taken the lead, and, up to the end of that first three-quarters of an hour, she found no inclination, on my part, to challenge her right to it.

I repeat, lest you did not get the full import of it, that I was a willing listener!

Now comes the part of the story which would make me blush with embarrassment, if it were not for the fact that you and I are separated by the pages of this book; but I must summon the courage with which to tell you the facts because the entire incident would lose its significance if I failed to do this.

As I have stated, my visitor entranced me with brilliant and captivating conversation for three-quarters of an hour. Now, what do you suppose she was talking about all that time?

No! You are wrong.

She was not trying to sell me a book, nor did she once use the personal pronoun "I."

However, she was not only trying, but actually selling me something, and that something was myself.

She had no sooner been seated in that big cushioned chair than she unrolled a package which I had mistaken for a book that she had come to sell me, and sure enough, there was a book in the package - in fact, several of them; for she had a complete year's file of the magazine of which I was then editor (Hill's Golden Rule). She turned the pages of those magazines and read places that she had marked here and there, assuring me, in the meanwhile, that she had always believed the philosophy back of that which she was reading.

Then, after I was in a state of complete mesmerism, and thoroughly receptive, my visitor tactfully switched the conversation to a subject which, I suspect, she had in mind to discuss with me long before she presented herself at my office; but - and this is another point at which most salespeople blunder - had she reversed the order of her conversation and begun where she finished, the chances are that she never would have had the opportunity to sit in that big easy-chair.

During the last three minutes of her visit, she skillfully laid before me the merits of some securities that she was selling. She did not ask me to purchase, but the way in which she told me of

8

the merits of the securities (plus the way in which she had so impressively told me of the merits of my own "game") had the psychological effect of causing me to want to purchase; and, even though I made no purchase of securities from her, she made a sale - because I picked up the telephone and introduced her to a man to whom she later sold more than five times the amount that she had intended selling me.

If that same woman, or another woman, or a man who had the tact and personality that she possessed should call on me, I would again sit down and listen for three-quarters of an hour.

We are all human, and we are all more or less vain!

We are all alike in this respect - we will listen with intense interest to those who have the tact to talk to us about that which lies closest to our hearts; and then, out of a sense of reciprocity, we will also listen with interest when the speaker finally switches the conversation to the subject which lies closest to his or her heart. And at the end, we will not only "sign on the dotted line" but we will say, "What a wonderful personality!"

In the city of Chicago, some years ago, I was conducting a school of salesmanship for a securities house which employed more than 1,500 salespeople. To keep the ranks of that big organization filled, we had to train and employ six hundred new salespeople every week. Of all the thousands of men and women who went through that school, there was but one man who grasped the significance of the principle I am here describing the first time he heard it analyzed.

This man had never tried to sell securities and frankly admitted, when he entered the salesmanship class, that he was not a salesman. Let's see whether he was or not.

After he had finished his training, one of the "star" salesmen took a notion to play a practical joke on him, believing him to be a credulous person who would believe all that he heard. So this "star" gave him an inside "tip" as to where he would be able to sell some securities without any great effort. This star would make the sale himself, so he said; but the man to whom he referred as being a likely purchaser was an ordinary artist who would purchase with so little urging that he, being a "star," did not wish to waste his time on him.

The newly made salesman was delighted to receive the "tip," and, forthwith, he was on his way to make the sale. As soon as he was out of the office, the "star" gathered the other "stars" around him and told of the joke he was playing. For in reality the artist was a very wealthy man and the "star," himself had spent nearly a month trying to sell him, but without success. It then developed that all of the "stars" of that particular group had called on this same artist but had failed to interest him.

The newly made salesman was gone about an hour and a half. When he returned he found the "stars" waiting for him with smiles on their faces.

To their surprise, the newly made salesman also wore a broad smile on his face. The "stars" looked at each other inquiringly, for they had expected that this "green" man would not return in a joyful mood.

"Well, did you sell to your man?" inquired the originator of this "joke."

"Certainly," replied the uninitiated one, "and I found that artist to be all you said he was - a perfect gentleman and a very interesting man."

Reaching into his pocket he pulled out an order and a check for $2,000.00.

The "stars" wanted to know how he did it.

"Oh, it wasn't difficult," replied the newly-made salesman; "I just walked in and talked to him a few minutes and he brought up the subject of the securities himself, and said he wanted to purchase; therefore, I really did not sell to him - he purchased of his own accord."

When I heard of the transaction, I called the newly-made salesman in and asked him to describe, in detail, just how he made the sale, and I will relate it just as he told it.

When he reached the artist's studio, he found him at work on a picture. So engaged in his work was the artist that he did not see the salesman enter, so the salesman walked over to where he could see the picture and stood there looking at it without saying a word.

Finally the artist saw him; then the salesman apologized for the intrusion and began to talk – about the picture that the artist was painting!

He knew just enough about art to be able to discuss the merits of the picture with some intelligence and he was really interested in the subject.

He liked the picture and frankly told the artist so, which, of course, made the artist very angry!

For nearly an hour those two men talked of nothing but art; particularly that picture that stood on the artist's easel.

Finally, the artist asked the salesman his name and his business, and the salesman (yes, the master salesman) replied, "Oh, never mind my business or my name. I am more interested in you and your art!"

The artist's face beamed with a smile of joy.

Those words fell as sweet music upon his ears. But, not to be outdone by his polite visitor, he insisted on knowing what mission had brought him to his studio.

Then, with an air of genuine reluctance, this master salesman - this real "star" - introduced himself and told his business.

Briefly he described the securities he was selling, and the artist listened as if he enjoyed every word that was spoken. After the salesman had finished the artist said:

"Well, well! I have been very foolish. Other salesmen from your firm have been here trying to sell me some of those securities, but they talked nothing but business; in fact, they annoyed me so that I had to ask one of them to leave. Now let me see - what was that fellow's name - oh, yes, it was Mr. Perkins." (Perkins was the "star" who had thought of this clever trick to play on the newly made salesman.) "But you present the matter so differently, and now I see how foolish I have been, and I want you to let me have $2,000.00 worth of those securities."

Think of that - "You present the matter so differently!"

And how did this newly made salesman present the matter so differently? Putting the question another way, what did this master salesman really sell that artist? Did he sell him securities?

No! He sold him his own picture which he was painting on his own canvas.

The securities were but an incident.

Don't overlook this point. That master salesman had remembered the story of the old lady who entertained me for three-quarters of an hour by talking about that which was nearest my heart, and it had so impressed him that he made up his mind to study his prospective purchasers and find out what would interest them most, so he could talk about that.

This "green," newly-made salesman earned $7,900.00 in commissions the first month he was in the field, leading the next highest man by more than double, and the tragedy of it was that not one person out of the entire organization of 1,500 salespeople took the time to find out how and why he became the real "star" of the organization - a fact which I believe fully justifies the rather biting reprimand suggested in Lesson Nine to which you may have taken offense.

A Carnegie, or a Rockefeller, or a James J. Hill, or a Marshall Field accumulates a fortune through the application of the selfsame principles that are available to all the remainder of us, but we envy them their wealth without ever thinking of studying their philosophy and appropriating it to our own use.

We look at a successful man in the hour of his triumph, and wonder how he did it, but we overlook the importance of analyzing his methods and we forget the price he had to pay in careful, well-organized preparation which had to be made before he could reap the fruits of his efforts.

Throughout this course on the Law of Success, you will not find a single new principle. Every one of them is as old as civilization itself. Yet you will find but few people who seem to understand how to apply them.

The salesman who sold those securities to that artist was not only a master salesman, but he was a man with an attractive personality. He was not much to look at; perhaps that is why the "star" conceived the idea of playing that cruel joke on him; but even a homely person may have a very attractive personality in the eyes of those whose handiwork he has praised.

Of course, there are some who will get the wrong conception of the principle I am here trying to make clear, by drawing the conclusion that any sort of cheap flattery will take the place of genuine heart interest. I hope that you are not one of these. I hope that you are one of those who understand the real psychology upon which this lesson is based, and that you will make it your business to study other people closely enough to find something about them or their work that you really admire. Only in this way can you develop a personality that will be irresistibly attractive.

Cheap flattery has just the opposite effect to that of constituting an attractive personality. It repels instead of attracting. It is so shallow that even the ignorant easily detect it.

· · · · · · · ·

Perhaps you have observed - and if you have not I wish you to do so - that this lesson emphasizes at length the importance of

12

making it your business to take a keen interest in other people and in their work, business or profession. This emphasis was by no means an accident.

. . . .

You will quickly observe that the principles upon which this lesson is based are very closely related to those which constitute the foundation of Lesson Six, on Imagination.

Also, you will observe that this lesson is based upon much the same general principles as those which form the most important part of Lesson Thirteen, on Co-operation.

Let us here introduce some very practical suggestions as to how the laws of Imagination, Co-operation and Pleasing Personality may be blended or coordinated to profitable ends, through the creation of usable ideas.

Every thinker knows that "ideas" are the beginning of all successful achievement. The question most often asked, however, is, "How can I learn to create ideas that will earn money?"

In part we will answer this question in this lesson by suggesting some new and novel ideas, any of which might be developed and made very profitable by almost anyone, in practically any locality.

IDEA NUMBER ONE

The world war has deprived Germany of her enormous trade in toys. Before the war we bought most of our toys from Germany. We are not likely to buy any more toys from German manufacturers in our time, or for a long while afterward.

Toys are in demand, not alone in the United States, but in foreign countries, many of which will not buy toys from Germany. Our only competitor is Japan and her toys are of so poor a quality that her competition means nothing.

But what sort of toys shall I manufacture and where will I get the capital with which to carry on the business, you will ask?

First, go to a local toy dealer and find out just which class of toys sells most rapidly. If you do not feel competent to make improvements on some of the toys now on the market, advertise for an inventor "with an idea for a marketable toy" and you will soon find the mechanical genius who will supply this missing link in your undertaking. Have him make you a working model of just what you want, then go to some small manufacturer, woodworker, machine shop or the like, and arrange to have your toys manufactured.

You now know just what your toy will cost, so you are ready to go to some big jobber, wholesaler or distributor and arrange for the sale of your entire product.

If you are an able salesman you can finance this whole project on the few dollars required with which to advertise for the inventor. When you find this man you can probably arrange with him to work out a model for you during his spare evening hours, with a promise that you will give him a better job when you are manufacturing your own toys. He will probably give you all the time you want in which to pay him for his labor; or he may do the work in return for an interest in the business.

You can get the manufacturer of your toys to wait for his money until you are paid by the firm to which you sell them, and if necessary, you can assign to him the invoices for the toys sold and let the money come direct to him.

Of course if you have an unusually pleasing and convincing personality and considerable ability to organize, you will be able to take the working model of your toy to some man of means and, in return for an interest in the business, secure the capital with which to do your own manufacturing.

If you want to know what will sell, watch a crowd of children at play, study their likes and dislikes, find out what will amuse them and you will probably get an idea on which to build your toy. It requires no genius to invent! Common sense is all that is necessary. Simply find out what the people want and then produce it. Produce it well - better than anyone else is doing. Give it a touch of individuality. Make it distinctive.

We spend millions of dollars annually for toys with which to entertain our children. Make your new toy useful as well as interesting. Make it educational if possible. If it entertains and teaches at the same time it will sell readily and live forever. If your toy is in the nature of a game make it teach the child something about the world in which it lives - geography, arithmetic, English, physiology, etc. Or, better still, produce a toy that will cause the child to run, jump or in some other way exercise. Children love to move about and moving about is of benefit to them, especially when stimulated by the play motive.

An indoor baseball game would be a ready seller, especially in the cities. Work out an arrangement for attaching the ball to a string that will be suspended from the ceiling so one child may throw the ball against the wall and then stand back and strike it with a bat as it rebounds. A one-child baseball game, in other words.

PLAN NUMBER TWO

This will be of interest only to the man or woman who has the self-confidence and the ambition to "run the risk" of making a big income, which, we may add, most people have not.

It is a suggestion that could be put into practical operation by at least forty or fifty people in every large city throughout the United States, and by a smaller number in the smaller cities.

It is intended for the man or woman who can write or will learn to write advertising copy, sales literature, follow-up letters, collection letters and the like, using the ability to write which we will suppose that you possess.

To make practical and profitable use of this suggestion you will need the co-operation of a good advertising agency and from one to five firms or individuals who do enough advertising to warrant their appropriations going through an agency.

You should go to the agency first and make arrangements with it to employ you and pay you seven per cent on the gross expenditures of all acounts which you bring to it; this seven per cent to compensate you for getting the account and for writing the copy and otherwise serving the client in the management of his advertising appropriation. Any reliable agency will gladly give you this amount for all the business you will bring.

Then you go to a firm or individual whose advertising account you wish to handle and say in effect that you wish to go to work without compensation. Tell what you can do and what you intend to do for that particular firm that will help it sell more goods. If the firm employs an advertising manager you are to become virtually his assistant without pay, on one condition: namely, that the advertising appropriation is to be placed through the agency with which you have the connection. Through this arrangement the firm or individual whose account you thus secure will get the benefit of your personal services, without cost, and pay no more for placing its advertising through your agency than it would through any other. If your canvass is convincing and you really take the time to prepare your case, you will get your account without much argument.

You can repeat this transaction until you have as many accounts as you can handle advantageously, which, under ordinary conditions, will be not more than ten or twelve; probably less if one or more of your clients spends upwards of $25,000.00 a year in advertising.

If you are a competent writer of advertising copy and have the ability to create new and profitable ideas for your clients you will be able to hold their business from year to year. You of course understand that you are not to accept more accounts than you can handle individually. You should spend a portion of your time in the place of business of each of your clients. In fact, you should have a desk and working equipment right on the grounds so you can get firsthand information as to your clients' sales problems, as well as accurate information as to their goods and wares.

Through this sort of effort you will give the advertising agency a reputation for effective service such as it would get in no other way, and you will please your clients because they will see satisfactory returns from your efforts. As long as you keep the agency and the clients whom you serve satisfied your job is safe and you will make money. A reasonable expectation of returns under this plan would be a gross business of $250,000.00 a year, on which your seven per cent would amount to $17,500.00.

A man or woman of unusual ability could run the figure much higher than this, up to, say, an income of $25,000.00 a year, while the tendency would be, however, to drop down to around $5,000.00 to $7,500.00, which are the figures that the "average" man or woman might reasonably expect to earn.

You can see that the plan has possibilities. It supplies independent work and gives you one hundred per cent of your earning power. It is better than a position as advertising manager, even if the position paid the same money, because it practically places you in a business of your own - one in which your name is constantly developing a survival value.

PLAN NUMBER THREE

This plan can be put into operation by almost any man or woman of average intelligence, and with but little preparation. Go to any first-class printer and make arrangements with him to handle all the business you bring to him, allowing you a commission of say ten per cent on the gross amount. Then go to the largest users of printed matter and get samples of everything in the way of printing that they use.

Form a partnership or working arrangement with a commercial artist who will go over all this printed matter and wherever suitable or appropriate he will improve the illustrations or make illustrations where none were used before, making a rough pencil sketch which can be pasted to the original printed matter.

Then, if you are not a writer of copy, form a working arrangement with someone who is and get him or her to go over the copy of the printed matter and improve it in every respect possible.

When the work is complete go back to the firm from whom you get the printed matter, taking with you quotations on the work and show what can be done in the way of improvement. Say nothing about your quotations, however, until you have shown how much you could improve the printed matter. You will probably get the entire business of that firm by giving that sort of service in connection with every job of printing it has done.

If you perform your service properly you will soon have all the business that your commercial artist, your copy writer and you can handle. It ought to be good for $5,000.00 a year apiece for you.

Any profits that you earn from the work of others in connection with any of these plans will be a legitimate profit - a profit to which you will be entitled in return for your ability to organize and bring together the necessary talent and ability with which to perform satisfactory service.

If you go into the toy business you will be entitled to a profit on the work of those who make the toys because it will be through your ability that employment for them is available.

It is more than likely that your brains and your ability, when added to that of those who work with you or for you, will greatly increase their earning capacity - even to the extent that they can well afford to see you make a small amount from their efforts because they will be still earning much more than they could earn without your guidance!

You are willing to take any of these plans and make a profit out of them, are you not? You see nothing wrong on your part, do you? If you are an employee, working for some other person or firm, may it not be possible that the head of that firm or that individual, with his ability to organize, finance, etc., is increasing your own earning capacity right now?

You want to get out of the employee class and become an employer. We do not blame you for that. Nearly every normal person wants to do the same. The one best first step to take is to serve the firm or individual for whom you are working just as you would wish to be served if you were that individual or the head of that firm.

Who are the big employers of help today? Are they the rich men's sons who fell heir to employer-ship? Not on your life! They are the men and women who came up from the ranks of the most lowly sort of labor; men and women who have had no greater opportunity than you have. They are in the positions that they hold because their superior ability has enabled them intelligently to direct others. You can acquire that ability if you will try.

Right in the town or city where you live there are people who probably could benefit by knowing you, and who could undoubtedly benefit you in return. In one section of the city lives John Smith who wishes to sell his grocery store and open a moving picture theater. In another section of the city is a man who has a moving picture theater that he would like to trade for a grocery store.

Can you bring them together?

If you can, you will serve both and earn a nice remuneration.

In your town or city are people who want the products raised on the farms in the surrounding community. On those farms are farmers who raise farm products and who want to get them into the hands of those who live in town. If you can find a way of carrying the farm products direct from the farm to the city or town consumer you will enable the farmer to get more for his products and the consumer to get those products for less, and still there will be a margin to pay you for your ingenuity in shortening the route between producer and consumer.

In business there are, broadly speaking, two classes of people - the Producers and the Consumers. The tendency of the times is to find some way of bringing these two together without so many intermediaries. Find a way to shorten the route between producer and consumer and you will have created a plan that will help these two classes and handsomely profit you.

The laborer is worthy of his hire. If you can create such a plan you are entitled to a fair proportion of that which you save for the consumer, and also a fair proportion of that which you make for the producer.

Let us warn you that whatever plan you create as a means of making money, you had better see that it slices off a little of the cost to the consumer instead of adding a little to that cost.

The business of bringing producer and consumer together is a profitable business when it is conducted fairly to both, and without a greedy desire to get all there is in sight! The American public is wonderfully patient with profiteers who impose upon it, but there is a pivotal point beyond which even the shrewdest of them dare not go.

It may be all right to corner the diamond market and run up enormously high the price of those white rocks which are dug out of the ground in Africa without trouble, but when the prices of food and clothing and other necessities begin to soar skyward there is a chance of someone getting into the bad graces of the American public.

If you crave wealth and are really brave enough to shoulder the burdens which go with it, reverse the usual method of acquiring it by giving your goods and wares to the world at the lowest possible profit you can afford instead of exacting all that you can with safety. Ford has found it profitable to pay his workers, not as little as he can get them for, but as much as his profits will permit. He has also found it profitable to reduce the price of his automobile to the consumer while other manufacturers (many of whom have long since failed) continued to increase their price.

There may be some perfectly good plans through the operation of which you could squeeze the consumer and still manage to keep out of jail, but you will enjoy much more peace of mind and in all probability more profits in the long run if your plan, when you complete it, is built along the Ford lines.

You have heard John D. Rockefeller abused considerably, but most of this abuse has been prompted by sheer envy upon the part of those who would like to have his money but who haven't the inclination to earn it. Regardless of your opinion of Rockefeller, do not forget that he began as a humble bookkeeper and that he gradually climbed to the top in the accumulation of money because of his ability to organize and direct other and less able men intelligently. This author can remember when he had to pay twenty-five cents for a gallon of lamp oil and walk two miles through the hot sun and carry it home in a tin can in the bargain. Now, Rockefeller's wagon will deliver it at the back door, in the city or on the farm, at a little over half that sum.

Who has a right to begrudge Rockefeller his millions as long as he has reduced the price of a needed commodity? He could just as easily have increased the price of lamp oil to half a dollar, but we seriously doubt that he would be a multi-millionaire today if he had done so.

There are a lot of us who want money, but ninety-nine out of every hundred who start to create a plan through which to get money give all their thought to the scheme through which to get hold of it and no thought to the service to be given in return for it.

A Pleasing Personality is one that makes use of Imagination and Co-operation. We have cited the foregoing illustrations of how ideas may be created to show you how to co-ordinate the laws of Imagination, Co-operation and a Pleasing Personality.

Analyze any man who does not have a Pleasing Personality and you will find lacking in that man the faculties of Imagination and Co-operation also.

This brings us to a suitable place at which to introduce one of the greatest lessons on personality ever placed on paper. It is also one of the most effective lessons on salesmanship ever written, for the subjects of attractive personality and salesmanship must always go hand in hand; they are inseparable.

I have reference to Shakespeare's masterpiece, Mark Antony's speech at the funeral of Caesar. Perhaps you have read this oration, but it is here presented with interpretations in parentheses which may help you to gather a new meaning from it.

The setting for that oration was something like the following:

Caesar is dead, and Brutus, his slayer, is called on to tell the Roman mob, that has gathered at the undertaker's, why he put Caesar out of the way. Picture, in your imagination, a howling mob that was none too friendly to Caesar, and that already believed that Brutus had done a noble deed by murdering him.

Brutus takes the platform and makes a short statement of his reasons for killing Caesar. Confident that he has won the day he takes his seat. His whole demeanor is that of one who believes his word will be accepted without question; it is one of haughtiness.

Mark Antony now takes the platform, knowing that the mob is antagonistic to him because he is a friend of Caesar. In a low, humble tone of voice Antony begins to speak:

Antony: "For Brutus' sake, I am beholding to you."
Fourth Citizen: "What does he say of Brutus?"
Third Citizen: "He says, for Brutus' sake, he finds himself beholding to us all."
Fourth Citizen: "'Twere best he speak no harm of Brutus here."
First Citizen: "This Caesar was a tyrant."
Third Citizen: "Nay, that's certain; we are blest that Rome is rid of him."
Second Citizen: "Peace! Let us hear what Antony can say." (Here you will observe, in Antony's opening sentence, his clever method of "neutralizing" the minds of his listeners.)
Antony: "You gentle Romans, -"
(About as "gentle" as a gang of Bolsheviks in a revolutionary labor meeting.)
All: "Peace, ho! Let us hear him."
(Had Antony begun his speech by "knocking" Brutus, the history of Rome would have been different.)
Antony: "Friends, Romans, Countrymen, lend me your ears;
I come to bury Caesar, not to praise him."
(Allying himself with what he knew to be the state of mind of his listeners.)
"The evil that men do lives after them;
The good is oft interred with their bones;
So let it be with Caesar. The noble Brutus
Hath told you Caesar was ambitious;
If it were so, it was a grievous fault;
And grievously bath Caesar answered it.
Here, under leave of Brutus and the rest, -
For Brutus is an honorable man;
So are they all, all honorable men -
Come I to speak at Caesar's funeral.
He was my friend - faithful, and just to me;
But Brutus says he was ambitious;
And Brutus is an honorable man;

21

He hath brought many captives home to Rome,
Whose ransoms did the general coffers fill;
Did this in Caesar seem ambitious?
When the poor have cried, Caesar hath wept;
Ambition should be made of sterner stuff;
Yet Brutus says he was ambitious;
And Brutus is an honorable man.
You all did see that on the Lupercal
I thrice presented him a kingly crown,
Which he did thrice refuse. Was this ambition?
Yet Brutus says he was ambitious;
And, surely, he is an honorable man.
I speak not to disprove what Brutus spoke,
But here I am to speak what I do know.
You all did love him once, not without cause;
What cause withholds you then to mourn for him?
O judgment! thou art fled to brutish beasts,
And men have lost their reason. Bear with me,
My heart is in the coffin there with Caesar,
And I must pause till it come back to me."

(At this point Antony paused to give his audience a chance to discuss hurriedly, among themselves, his opening statements. His object in doing this was to observe what effect his words were having, just as a master salesman always encourages his prospective purchaser to talk so he may know what is in his mind.)

First Citizen: "Me thinks there is much in his sayings"
Second Citizen: "If thou consider rightly of the matter, Caesar has
    had great wrong."
Third Citizen: "Has he, masters? I fear there will be worse come in
    his place."
Fourth Citizen: "Mark'd ye his words? He would not take the
    crown? Therefore 'tis certain he was not ambitious."
First Citizen: "If it be found so, someone will dear abide it."
Second Citizen: "Poor soul! His eyes are red as fire with weeping."
Third Citizen: "There's not a nobler man in Rome than Antony."
Fourth Citizen: "Now mark him, he begins again to speak".
Antony: "But yesterday the word of Caesar might
    Have stood against the world; now lies he there,
    And none so poor to do him reverence.

O masters (appealing to their vanity) if I were disposed to
    stir
Your hearts and minds to mutiny and rage,
I should do Brutus wrong and Cassius wrong,
Who, you all know, are honorable men."

(Observe how often Antony has repeated the term
"honorable." Observe, also, how cleverly he brings in the first
suggestion that, perhaps, Brutus and Cassius may not be as
honorable as the Roman mob believes them to be. This suggestion
is carried in the words "mutiny" and "rage" which he here uses for
the first time, after his pause gave him time to observe that the
mob was swinging over toward his side of the argument. Observe
how carefully he is "feeling" his way and making his words fit that
which he knows to be the frame of mind of his listeners.)

Antony: "I will not do them wrong; I rather choose
    To wrong the dead, to wrong myself and you,
    Than I will wrong such honorable men."

(Crystallizing his suggestion into hatred of Brutus and
Cassius, he then appeals to their curiosity and begins to lay the
foundation for his climax - a climax which he knows will win the
mob because he is reaching it so cleverly that the mob believes it
to be its own conclusion.)

Antony: "But here's a parchment, with the seal of Caesar;
    I found it in his closet; 'tis his will;
    Let but the commons hear this testament,
    Which, pardon me, I do not mean to read -"

(Tightening up on his appeal to their curiosity by making
them believe he does not intend to read the will.)

    "And they would go and kiss dead Caesar's wounds
    And dip their napkins in his sacred blood,
    Yea, beg a hair of him for memory,
    And, dying, mention it within their wills,
    Bequeathing it as a rich legacy
    Unto their issue."

(Human nature always wants that which is difficult to get,
or that of which it is about to be deprived. Observe how craftily
Antony has awakened the interest of the mob and made them
want to hear the reading of the will, thereby preparing them to

hear it with open minds. This marks his second step in the process of "neutralizing" their minds.)

All: "The will, the will! We will hear Caesar's will."

Antony: "Have patience, gentle friends, I must not read it;
It is not meet you know how Caesar loved you.
You are not wood, you are not stones, but men;
And, being men, hearing the will of Caesar,
It will inflame you; (Exactly what he wishes to do)
It will make you mad;
'Tis good you know not that you are his heirs,
For if you should, O what will come of it!"

Fourth Citizen: "Read the will; we'll hear it,

Antony: You shall read us the will; Caesar's will."

Antony: "Will you be patient? Will you stay awhile?
I have o'ershot myself to tell you of it;
I fear I wrong the honorable men
Whose daggers have stabb'd Caesar, I do fear it."

("Daggers" and "stabb'd" suggest cruel murder. Observe how cleverly Antony injects this suggestion into his speech, and observe, also, how quickly the mob catches its significance, because, unknown to the mob, Antony has carefully prepared their minds to receive this suggestion.)

Fourth Citizen: "They were traitors, honorable men!"

All: "The will! The testament!"

Second Citizen: "They were villains, murderers; the will!" (Just what Antony would have said in the beginning, but he knew it would have a more desirable effect if he planted the thought in the minds of the mob and permitted them to say it themselves.)

Antony: "You will compel me then to read the will?
Then make a ring about the corpse of Caesar,
And let me show you him that made the will.
Shall I descend, and will you give me leave?"

(This was the point at which Brutus should have begun to look for a back door through which to make his escape.)

All: "Come down."

Second Citizen: "Descend."

Third Citizen: "Room for Antony, most noble Antony."
Antony: "Nay, press not so upon me, stand far off."

(He knew this command would make them want to draw
nearer, which is what he wanted them to do.)

All: "Stand back. Room."
Antony: "If you have tears, prepare to shed them now. You all do
      know this mantle; I remember
      The first time ever Caesar put it on;
      'Twas on a summer's evening, in his tent,
      That day he overcame the Nervii;
      Look, in this place ran Cassius' dagger through;
      See what a rent the envious Casca made;
      Through this the well-beloved Brutus stabb'd;
      And as he plucked his cursed steel away,
      Mark how the blood of Caesar followed it,
      As rushing out of doors, to be resolved
      If Brutus so unkindly knock'd or no;
      For Brutus, as you know, was Caesar's angel;
      Judge, O you gods, how dearly Caesar loved him!
      This was the most unkindest cut of all;
      For, when the noble Caesar saw him stab,
      Ingratitude, more strong than traitor's arms,
      Quite vanquish'd him; then burst his mighty heart;
      And, in his mantle muffling up his face,
      Even at the base of Pompey's statua,
      Which all the while ran blood, great Caesar fell.
      O, what a fall was there, my countrymen!
      Then I, and you, and all of us fell down
      While bloody treason flourish'd over us.
      O, now you weep, and I perceive you feel
      The dint of pity; these are gracious drops.
      Kind soul, why weep you when you but behold
      Our Caesar's vesture wounded? Look you here;
      Here is himself, marr'd, as you see, with traitors."

(Observe how Antony now uses the words "traitors" quite
freely, because he knows that it is in harmony with that which is in
the minds of the Roman mob.)

First Citizen: "O piteous spectacle!"
Second Citizen: "O woeful day!"
Third Citizen: "O woeful day!"
First Citizen: "O most bloody sight!"
Second Citizen: "We will be revenged."

(Had Brutus been a wise man instead of a braggart he would have been many miles from the scene by this tune.)

All: "Revenge! About! Seek! Burn! Fire! Kill! Slay! Let not a traitor live!"

(Here Antony takes the next step toward crystallizing the frenzy of the mob into action; but, clever salesman that he is, does not try to force this action.)
Antony: "Stay, countrymen."
First Citizen: "Peace there! Hear the noble Antony."
Second Citizen: "We'll hear him, we'll follow him, we'll die with him."

(From these words Antony knows that he has the mob with him. Observe how he takes advantage of this psychological moment - the moment for which all master salesmen wait.)

Antony: "Good friends, sweet friends, let me not stir you up to such a sudden flood of mutiny.
They that have done this deed are honorable.
What private griefs they have, alas, I know not,
That made them do it; they were wise and honorable,
And will, no doubt, with reasons answer you.
I come not, friends, to steal away your hearts:
I am no orator as Brutus is;
But, as you know me all, a plain, blunt man,
That love my friend; and that they know full well
That gave me public leave to speak of him;
For I have neither wit, nor words, nor worth,
Action, nor utterance, nor the power of speech,
To stir men's blood; I only speak right on;
I tell you that which you yourselves do know;
Show you sweet Caesar's wounds, poor, poor, dumb mouths.

26

And bid them speak for me; but were I Brutus,
And Brutus Antony, there an Antony
Would ruffle up your spirits, and put a tongue
In every wound of Caesar that should move
The stones of Rome to rise and mutiny."
All: "We'll mutiny."
First Citizen: "We'll burn the house of Brutus."
Third Citizen: "Away, then! Come, seek the conspirators."
Antony: "Yet hear me, countrymen; yet hear me speak!"
All: "Peace, ho! Hear Antony. Most noble Antony!"
Antony: "Why, friends, you go to do you know not what;
Wherein hath Caesar thus deserved your love?
Alas, you know not; I must tell you, then;
You have forgot the will I told you of."

(Antony is now ready to play his trump card; he is ready to reach his climax. Observe how well he has marshaled his suggestions, step by step, saving until the last his most important statement; the one on which he relied for action. In the great field of salesmanship and in public speaking many a man tries to reach this point too son, tries to "rush" his audience or his prospective purchaser, and thereby loses his appeal.)

All: "Most true; the will! Let's stay and hear the will."
Antony: "Here is the will, and under Caesar's seal.
To every Roman citizen he gives,
To every several man, seventy-five drachmas."
Second Citizen: "Most noble Caesar! we'll revenge his death."
Third Citizen: "O royal Caesar!"
Antony: "Hear me with patience."
All: "Peace, ho! "
Antony: "Moreover, he hath left you all his walks,His private
arbors and new planted orchards,
On this side Tiber; he hath left them you,
And to your heirs forever; common pleasures,
To walk abroad and recreate yourself.
Here was a Caesar! When comes such another?"
First Citizen: "Never, never. Come, away, away!
We'll burn his body in the holy place,
And with the brands fire the traitors' houses.
Take up the body."

Second Citizen: "Go fetch fire."
Third Citizen: "Pluck down benches."
Fourth Citizen: "Pluck down forms, windows, anything."

And that was Brutus' finish!

He lost his case because he lacked the personality and the good judgment with which to present his argument from the viewpoint of the Roman mob, as Mark Antony did. His whole attitude clearly indicated that he thought pretty well of himself, that he was proud of his deed. We have all seen people, in this day and time, who somewhat resemble Brutus in this respect, but, if we observe closely, we notice that they do not accomplish very much.

Suppose that Mark Antony had mounted the platform in a "strutting" attitude, and had begun his speech in this wise:

"Now let me tell you Romans something about this man Brutus - he is a murderer at heart and - " he would have gone no further, for the mob would have howled him down.

Clever salesman and practical psychologist that he was, Mark Antony so presented his case that it appeared not to be his own idea at all, but that of the Roman mob itself.

Go back to the lesson on initiative and leadership and read it again, and as you read, compare the psychology of it with that of Mark Antony's speech. Observe how the "you" and not "I" attitude toward others was emphasized. Observe, if you please, how this same point is emphasized throughout this course, and especially in Lesson Seven, on enthusiasm.

Shakespeare was, by far, the most able psychologist and writer known to civilization; for that reason, all of his writings are based upon unerring knowledge of the human mind. Throughout this speech, which he placed in the mouth of Mark Antony, you will observe how carefully he assumed the "you" attitude; so carefully that the Roman mob was sure that its decision was of its own making.

I must call your attention, however, to the fact that Mark Antony's appeal to the self-interest of the Roman mob was of the crafty type, and was based upon the stealth with which dishonest men often make use of this principle in appealing to the cupidity and avarice of their victims. While Mark Antony displayed evidence of great self-control in being able to assume, at the beginning of his speech, an attitude toward Brutus that was not

28

real, at the same time it is obvious that his entire appeal was based upon his knowledge of how to influence the minds of the Roman mob through flattery.

The two letters reproduced in Lesson Seven of this course illustrate, in a very concrete way, the value of the "you" and the fatality of the "I" appeal. Go back and read these letters again and observe how the more successful of the two follows closely the Mark Antony appeal, while the other one is based upon an appeal of just the opposite nature. Whether you are writing a sales letter, or preaching a sermon or writing an advertisement or a book, you will do well to follow the same principles employed by Mark Antony in his famous speech.

Now let us turn our attention to the study of ways and means through which one may develop a pleasing personality.

Let us start with the first essential, which is character, for no one may have a pleasing personality without the foundation of a sound, positive character. Through the principle of telepathy you "telegraph" the nature of your character to those with whom you come in contact, which is responsible for what you have often called an "intuitive" feeling that the person whom you had just met but about whom you did not know very much, was not trustworthy.

You may embellish yourself with clothes of the neatest and latest design, and conduct yourself in a most pleasing manner as far as outside appearances go, but if there is greed, and envy, and hatred, and jealousy, and avarice, and selfishness in your heart, you will never attract any, except those characters which harmonize with your own. Like attracts like, and you may be sure therefore, that those who are attracted to you are those whose inward natures parallel your own.

You may embellish yourself with an artificial smile that belies your feelings, and you may practice the art of handshaking so that you can imitate, perfectly, the handshake of the person who is adept at this art, but if these outward manifestations of an attractive personality lack that vital factor called earnestness of purpose, they will repel instead of attract.

How, then, may one build character?

The first step in character building is rigid self-discipline.

In both the second and eighth lessons of this course, you will find the formula through which you may shape your character after any pattern that you cose, but I repeat it here, as it is based upon a principle that will bear much repetition, as follows:

First: Select those whose characters were made up of the qualities which you wish to build into your own character, and then proceed, in the manner described in Lesson Two, to appropriate these qualities through the aid of Auto-suggestion. Create in your imagination a council table and gather your characters around it each night, first having written out a clear, concise statement of the particular qualities that you wish to appropriate from each. Then proceed to affirm or suggest to yourself, in outspoken, audible words, that you are developing the desired qualities in yourself. As you do this close your eyes and see in your imagination the figures seated around your imaginary table, in the manner described in Lesson Two.

Second: Through the principles described in Lesson Eight on self-control, control your thoughts and keep your mind vitalized with thoughts of a positive nature. Let the dominating thought of your mind be a picture of the person that you intend to be; the person that you are deliberately building through this procedure. At least a dozen times a day, when you have a few minutes to yourself, shut your eyes and direct your thoughts to the figures which you have selected to sit at your imaginary council table, and feel, with a faith that knows NO LIMITATION, that you are actually growing to resemble in character those figures of your choice.

Third: Find at least one person each day, and more if possible, in whom you see some good quality that is worthy of praise, and praise it. Remember, however, that this praise must not be in the nature of cheap, insincere flattery; it must be genuine. Speak your words of praise with such earnestness that they will impress those to whom you speak. Then watch what happens. You will have rendered those whom you praise a decided benefit of great value to them, and you will have gone just one more step in the direction of developing the habit of looking for and finding the good qualities in others. I cannot overemphasize the far-reaching effects of this habit of praising, openly and enthusiastically, the good qualities in others; for this habit will soon reward you with a feeling of self-respect and manifestation of gratitude from others that will modify your entire personality. Here, again, the law of attraction enters, and those whom you praise will see in you the qualities that you see in them. Your

30

success in the application of this formula will be in exact proportion to your faith in its soundness.

I do not merely believe that it is sound - I know that it is - and the reason I know is that I have used it successfully and I have also taught others how to use it successfully. Therefore, I have a right to promise you that you can use it with equal success.

Furthermore, you can, with the aid of this formula, develop an attractive personality so speedily that you will surprise all who know you. The development of such a personality is entirely within your own control, a fact which gives you a tremendous advantage and at the same time places upon you the responsibility if you fail or neglect to exercise your privilege.

I now wish to direct your attention to the reason for speaking aloud the affirmation that you are developing the desired qualities which you have selected as the materials out of which to develop an attractive personality.

This procedure has two desirable effects, namely-

First: It sets into motion the vibration through which the thought back of your words reaches and imbeds itself in your subconscious mind, where it takes root and grows until it becomes a great moving force in your outward, physical activities, leading in the direction of transformation of the thought into reality.

Second: It develops in you the ability to speak with force and conviction which will lead, finally, to great ability as a public speaker. No matter what your calling in life may be, you should be able to stand upon your feet and speak convincingly, as this is one of the most effective ways of developing an attractive personality.

Put feeling and emotion into your words as you speak, and develop a deep, rich tone of voice. If your voice is inclined to be high pitched, tone it down until it is soft and pleasing. You can never express an attractive personality to best advantage through a harsh or shrill voice. You must cultivate your voice until it becomes rhythmical and pleasing to the ear.

Remember that speech is the chief method of expressing your personality, and for this reason it is to your advantage to cultivate a style that is both forceful and pleasing.

I do not recall a single outstanding attractive personality that was not made up, in part, of ability to speak with force and conviction. Study the prominent men and women of today, wherever you find them, and observe the significant fact that the more prominent they are, the more efficient are they in speaking forcefully.

Study the outstanding figures of the past in politics and statesmanship and observe that the most successful ones were those who were noted for their ability to speak with force and conviction.

In the field of business, industry and finance, it seems significant also that the most prominent leaders are men and women who are able public speakers.

In fact, no one may hope to become a prominent leader in any noteworthy undertaking without developing the ability to speak with forcefulness that carries conviction. While the salesman may never deliver a public address, he will profit nevertheless if he develops the ability to do so, because this ability increases his power to talk convincingly in ordinary conversation.

Let us now summarize the chief factors which enter into the development of an attractive personality, as follows:

First: Form the habit of interesting yourself in other people, and make it your business to find their good qualities and speak of them in terms of praise.

Second: Develop the ability to speak with force and conviction, both in your ordinary conversational tones and before public gatherings where you must use more volume.

Third: Clothe yourself in a style that is becoming to your physical build and the work in which you are engaged.

Fourth: Develop a positive character, through the aid of the formula outlined in this lesson.

Fifth: Learn how to shake hands so that you express warmth of feeling and enthusiasm through this form of greeting.

Sixth: Attract other people to you by first "attracting yourself" to them.

Seventh: Remember that your only limitation, within reason, is the one which YOU set up in YOUR OWN mind.

These seven points cover the most important factors that enter into the development of an attractive personality, but it seems hardly necessary to suggest that such a personality will not develop of its own accord. It will develop if you submit yourself to the discipline herein described with a firm determination to transform yourself into the person that you would like to be.

As I study this list of seven important factors that enter into the development of an attractive personality, I feel moved to direct your attention to the second and the fourth as being the most important.

If you will cultivate those finer thoughts and feelings and actions out of which a positive character is built, and then learn to express yourself with force and conviction, you will have developed an attractive personality - for it will be seen that out of this attainment will come the other qualities here outlined.

There is a great power of attraction back of the person who has a positive character, and this power expresses itself through unseen as well as visible sources. The moment you come within speaking distance of such a person, even though not a word is spoken, the influence of the "unseen power within" makes itself felt.

Every "shady" transaction in which you engage, every negative thought that you think, and every destructive act in which you indulge, destroys just so much of that "subtle something" within you that is known as character.

"There is full confession in the glances of our eyes; in our smiles; in salutations; in the grasp of the hands. His sin bedaubs him, mars all his good impression. Men know not why they do not trust him, but they do not trust him. His vice glasses his eye, demeans his cheek, pinches the nose, sets the mark of beast on the back of the head, and writes, 'O fool! fool!' on the forehead of a king." (Emerson.)

I would direct your attention, now, to the first of the seven factors that enter into the development of an attractive personality. You have observed that all through this lesson I have gone into lengthy detail to show the material advantages of being agreeable to other people.

However, the biggest advantage of all lies not in the possibility of monetary or material gain which this habit offers, but in the beautifying effect that it has upon the character of all who practice it.

Acquire the habit of making yourself agreeable and you profit both materially and mentally; for you will never be as happy in any other way as you will be when you know that you are making others happy.

Remove the chips from your shoulders and quit challenging men to engage you in useless arguments! Remove the smoked glasses through which you see what you believe to be the "blueness" of life and behold the shining sunlight of friendliness in its stead. Throw away your hammer and quit knocking, for surely you must know that the big prizes of life go to the builders and not the destroyers.

The man who builds a house is an artist; the man who tears it down is a junkman. If you are a person with a grievance, the world will listen to your vitriolic "ravings," providing it does not "see you coming"; but, if you are a person with a message of friendliness and optimism, it will listen because it wishes to do so.

No person with a grievance can be also a person with an attractive personality!

The art of being agreeable -
- Just that one simple trait -
- is the very foundation of all successful salesmanship.

I drive my automobile five miles into the outskirts of the city to purchase gasoline which I could procure within two blocks of my own garage because the man who runs the filling station is an artist; he makes it his business to be agreeable. I go there, not because he has cheaper gasoline, but because I enjoy the vitalizing effect of his attractive personality!

I buy shoes at Fiftieth Street and Broadway, in New York, not because I cannot find other good shoes at the same price, but for the reason that Mr. Cobb, the manager of that particular Regal Store, has an attractive personality. While he is fitting me with shoes, he makes it his business to talk to me on subjects which he knows to be close to my heart.

I do my banking at the Harriman National Bank, at Forty-fourth Street and Fifth Avenue, not because there are not scores of other good banks much nearer my place of business; but for the reason that the tellers, and the cashiers, and the lobby detective, and Mr. Harriman, and all of the others with whom I come in contact, make it their business to be agreeable. My account is small but they receive me as though it were large.

I greatly admire John D. Rockefeller, Jr., not because he is the son of one of the world's richest men, but for the better reason that he, too, has acquired the art of being agreeable.

In the little city of Lancaster, Pennsylvania, lives M. T. Garvin, a very successful merchant whom I would travel hundreds of miles to visit, not because he is a wealthy merchant, but for the reason that he makes it his business to be agreeable. However, I have no doubt that his material success is closely related to this noble art of affability which he has acquired.

I have in my vest pocket a Parker fountain pen, and my wife and children have pens of the same brand, not because there are not other good fountain pens, but for the reason that I have been attracted to George S. Parker on account of his habit of being agreeable.

My wife takes the Ladies' Home Journal, not because there are not other good magazines of a similar nature, but for the reason that we became attracted to the journal several years ago, while Edward Bok was its editor, because he had acquired the art of being agreeable.

O ye struggling pilgrims, who are searching for the rainbow's end; ye drawers of water and hewers of wood, tarry for a moment by the wayside and learn a lesson from the successful men and women who have succeeded because they acquired the art of being agreeable!

You can win, for a time, through ruthlessness and stealth; you can garner in more of this world's goods than you will need by sheer force and shrewd strategy, without taking the time or going to the trouble of being agreeable; but, sooner or later, you will come to that point in life at which you will feel the pangs of remorse and the emptiness of your well-filled purse.

I never think of power and position and wealth that was attained by force, without feeling - very deeply - the sentiment expressed by a man whose name I dare not mention, as he stood at the tomb of Napoleon:

"A little while ago I stood by the grave of the old Napoleon - a magnificent tomb of gilt and gold, fit almost for a deity dead - and gazed upon the sarcophagus of rare and nameless marble, where rest at last the ashes of that restless man. I leaned over the balustrade and thought about the career of the greatest soldier of the modem world. I saw him at Toulon. I saw him walking upon the banks of the Seine contemplating suicide. I saw him putting down the mob in the streets of Paris. I saw him at the head of the army in Italy. I saw him crossing the bridge at Lodi with the tri-color in his hand. I saw him in Egypt, in the shadows of the pyramids; I saw him conquer the Alps and mingle the eagles of France with the eagles of the crags. I saw him at Marengo, at Ulm and at Austerlitz. I saw him in Russia, when the infantry of the snow and the cavalry of the wild blast scattered his legions like winter's withered leaves. I saw him at Leipsic in defeat and disaster - driven by a million bayonets back upon Paris - clutched like a wild beast - banished to Elba. I saw him escape and re-take an empire by the force of his genius. I saw him upon the frightful field of Waterloo, where chance and fate combined to wreck the fortunes of their former king. And I saw him at St. Helena, with his hands crossed behind him, gazing out upon the sad and solemn sea.

I thought of the widows and orphans he had made, of the tears that had been shed for his glory, and of the only woman who ever loved him, pushed from his heart by the cold hand of ambition. And I said I would rather have been a French peasant and worn wooden shoes; I would rather have lived in a hut with a vine growing over the door, and the grapes growing purple in the amorous kisses of the autumn sun; I would rather have been that poor peasant, with my wife by my side knitting as the day died out of the sky, with my children upon my knees and their arms about me; I would rather have been this man and gone down to the tongueless silence of the dreamless dust, than to have been that imperial personation of force and murder, known as Napoleon the Great."

I leave with you, as a fitting climax for this lesson, the thought of this deathless dissertation on a man who lived by the sword of force and died an ignominious death, an outcast in the eyes of his fellow men, a sore to the memory of civilization, a failure because -

He did not acquire the art of being agreeable! Because he could not or would not subordinate "self" for the good of his followers.

Lesson Eleven

ACCURATE THOUGHT

"You Can Do It if You Believe You Can!"

THIS is at one and the same time the most important, the most interesting and the most difficult to present lesson of this entire course on the Law of Success.

It is important because it deals with a principle which runs through the entire course. It is interesting for the same reason. It is difficult to present for the reason that it will carry the average student far beyond the boundary line of his common experiences and into a realm of thought in which he is not accustomed to dwell.

Unless you study this lesson with an open mind, you will miss the very key-stone to the arch of this course, and without this stone you can never complete your Temple of Success.

This lesson will bring you a conception of thought which may carry you far above the level to which you have risen by the evolutionary processes to which you have been subjected in the past; and, for this reason, you should not be disappointed if, at firstreading, you do not fully understand it. Most of us disbelieve that which we cannot understand, and it is with knowledge of this human tendency in mind that I caution you against closing your mind if you do not grasp all that is in this lesson at the first reading.

For thousands of years men made ships of wood, and of nothing else. They used wood because they believed that it was the only substance that would float; but that was because they had not yet advanced far enough in their thinking process to understand the truth that steel will float, and that it is far superior to wood for the building of ships. They did not know that anything could float which was lighter than the amount of water is displaced, and until they learned of this great truth they went on making ships of wood.

Until some twenty-five years ago, most men thought that only the birds could fly, but now we know that man can not only equal the flying of the birds, but he can excel it.

Men did not know, until quite recently, that the great open void known as the air is more alive and more sensitive than anything that is on the earth. They did not know that the spoken word would travel through the ether with the speed of a flash of lightning, without the aid of wires. How could they know this when their minds had not been unfolded sufficiently to enable them to grasp it? The purpose of this lesson is to aid you in so unfolding and expanding your mind that you will be able to think with accuracy, for this unfoldment will open to you a door that leads to all the power you will need in completing your Temple of Success.

All through the preceding lessons of this course you observed that we have dealt with principles which any one could easily grasp and apply. You will also observe that these principles have been so presented that they lead to success as measured by material wealth. This seemed necessary for the reason that to most people the word success and the word money are synonymous terms. Obviously, the previous lessons of this course were intended for those who look upon worldly things and material wealth as being all that there is to success.

Presenting the matter in another way, I was conscious of the fact that the majority of the students of this course would feel disappointed if I pointed out to them a roadway to success that leads through other than the doorways of business, and finance, and industry; for it is a matter of common knowledge that most men want success that is spelled $UCCE$$!

Very well - let those who are satisfied with this standard of success have it; but some there are who will want to go higher up the ladder, in search of success which is measured in other than material standards, and it is for their benefit in particular that this and the subsequent lessons of this course are intended.
· · · · · · · ·

Accurate thought involves two fundamentals which all who indulge in it must observe. First, to think accurately you must separate facts from mere information. There is much "information" available to you that is not based upon facts. Second, you must separate facts into two classes; namely, the importantand the unimportant, or, the relevant and the irrelevant. Only by so doing can you think clearly.

All facts which you can use in the attainment of your definite chief aim are important and relevant; all that you cannot use are unimportant and irrelevant. It is mainly the neglect of some to make this distinction which accounts for the chasm which separates so widely people who appear to have equal ability, and who have had equal opportunity. Without going outside of your own circle of acquaintances you can point to one or more persons who have had no greater opportunity than you have had, and who appear to have no more, and perhaps less, ability than you, who are achieving far greater success.

And you wonder why!

Search diligently and you will discover that all such people have acquired the habit of combining and using the important facts which affect their line of work. Far from working harder than you, they are perhaps working less and with greater ease. By virtue of their having learned the secret of separating the important facts from the unimportant, they have provided themselves with a sort of fulcrum and lever with which they can move with their little fingers loads that you cannot budge with the entire weight of your body.

The person who forms the habit of directing his attention to the important facts out of which he is constructing his Temple of Success, thereby provides himself with a power which may be likened to a trip-hammer which strikes a ten-ton blow as compared to a tack-hammer which strikes a one-pound blow!

If these similes appear to be elementary you mustkeep in mind the fact that some of the students of this course have not yet developed the capacity to think in more complicated terms, and to try to force them to do so would be the equivalent of leaving them hopelessly behind.

That you may understand the importance of distinguishing between facts and mere information, study that type of man who is guided entirely by that which he hears; the type who is influenced by all the "whisperings of the winds of gossip"; that accepts, without analysis, all that he reads in the newspapers and judges others by what their enemies and competitors and contemporaries say about them.

Search your circle of acquaintances and pick out one of this type as an example to keep before your mind while we are on this subject. Observe that this man usually begins his conversation with some such term as this - "I see by the papers," or "they say." The accurate thinker knows that the newspapers are not always accurate in their reports, and he also knows that what "they say" usually carries more falsehood than truth. If you have not risen above the "I see by the papers," and the "they say" class, you have still far to go before you become an accurate thinker. Of course, much truth and many facts travel in the guise of idle gossip and newspaper reports; but the accurate thinker will not accept as such all that he sees and hears.

This is a point which I feel impelled to emphasize, for the reason that it constitutes the rocks and reefs on which so many people flounder and go down to defeat in a bottomless ocean of false conclusions.

In the realm of legal procedure, there is a principle which is called the law of evidence; and the object of this law is to get at the facts. Any judge can proceed with justice to all concerned, if he has the facts upon which to base his judgment, but he may play havoc with innocent people if he circumvents the law of evidence and reaches a conclusion or judgment that is based upon hearsay information. The law of Evidence varies according to the subject and circumstances with which it is used, but you will not go far wrong if, in the absence of that which you know to be facts, you form your judgments on the hypothesis that only that part of the evidence before you which furthers your own interests without working any hardship on others is based upon facts.

This is a crucial and important point in this lesson; therefore, I wish to be sure that you do not pass it by lightly. Many a man mistakes, knowingly or otherwise, expediency for fact; doing a thing, or refraining from doing it, for the sole reason that his action furthers his own interest without consideration as to whether it interferes with the rights of others.

No matter how regrettable, it is true that most thinking of today, far from being accurate, is based upon the sole foundation of expediency. It is amazing to the more advanced student of accurate thought, how many people there are who are "honest" when it is profitable to them, but find myriads of facts (?) to justify themselves in following a dishonest course when that course seems to be more profitable or advantageous.

No doubt you know people who are like that.

The accurate thinker adopts a standard by which he guides himself, and he follows that standard at alltimes, whether it works always to his immediate advantage, or carries him, now and then, through the fields of disadvantage (as it undoubtedly will).

The accurate thinker deals with facts, regardless of how they affect his own interests, for he knows that ultimately this policy will bring him out on top, in full possession of the object of his definite chief aim in life. He understands the soundness of the philosophy that the old philosopher, Croesus, had in mind when he said: "There is a wheel on which the affairs of men revolve, and its mechanism is such that it prevents any man from being always fortunate."

The accurate thinker has but one standard by which he conducts himself, in his intercourse with his fellow men, and that standard is observed by him as faithfully when it brings him temporary disadvantage as it is when it brings him outstanding advantage; for, being an accurate thinker, he knows that, by the law of averages, he will more than regain at some future time that which he loses by applying his standard to his own temporary detriment.

You might as well begin to prepare yourself to understand that it requires the staunchest and most unshakable character to become an accurate thinker, for you can see that this is where the reasoning of this lesson is leading.

There is a certain amount of temporary penalty attached to accurate thinking; there is no denying this fact; but, while this is true, it is also true that the compensating reward, in the aggregate, is so overwhelmingly greater that you will gladly pay this penalty.

In searching for facts it is often necessary to gather them through the sole source of knowledge and experience of others. It then becomes necessary to examine carefully both the evidence submitted and the person from whom the evidence comes; and when the evidence is of such a nature that it affects the interest of the witness who is giving it, there will be reason to scrutinize it all the more carefully, as witnesses who have an interest in the evidence that they are submitting often yield to the temptation to color and pervert it to protect that interest.

If one man slanders another, his remarks should be accepted, if of any weight at all, with at least a grain of the proverbial salt of caution; for it is a common human tendency for men to find nothing but evil in those whom they do not like. The man who has attained to the degree of accurate thinking that enables him to speak of his enemy without exaggerating his faults, and minimizing his virtues, is the exception and not the rule.

Some very able men have not yet risen above this vulgar and self-destructive habit of belittling their enemies, competitors and contemporaries. I wish to bring this common tendency to your attention with all possible emphasis, because it is a tendency that is fatal to accurate thinking.

Before you can become an accurate thinker, you must understand and make allowance for the fact that the moment a man or a woman begins to assume leadership in any walk of life, the slanderers begin to circulate "rumors" and subtle whisperings reflecting upon his or her character.

No matter how fine one's character is or whatservice he may be engaged in rendering to the world, he cannot escape the notice of those misguided people who delight in destroying instead of building. Lincoln's political enemies circulated the report that he lived with a colored woman. Washington's political enemies circulated a similar report concerning him. Since both Lincoln and Washington were southern men, this report was undoubtedly regarded by those who circulated it as being at one and the same time the most fitting and degrading one they could imagine.

But we do not have to go back to our first President to find evidence of this slanderous nature with which men are gifted, for they went a step further, in paying their tributes to the late President Harding, and circulated the report that he had negro blood in his veins.

When Woodrow Wilson came back from Paris with what he believed to be a sound plan for abolishing war and settling international disputes, all except the accurate thinker might have been led to believe, by the reports of the "they say" chorus, that he was a combination of Nero and Judas Iscariot. The little politicians, and the cheap politicians, and the "interest-paid" politicians, and the plain ignorants who did no thinking of their own, all joined in one mighty chorus for the purpose of destroying the one and only man in the history of the world who offered a plan for abolishing war.

The slanderers killed both Harding and Wilson - murdered them with vicious lies. They did the same to Lincoln, only in a somewhat more spectacular manner, by inciting a fanatic to hasten his death with a bullet.

Statesmanship and politics are not the only fieldsin which the accurate thinker must be on guard against the "they say" chorus. The moment a man begins to make himself felt in the field of industry or business, this chorus becomes active. If a man makes a better mouse-trap than his neighbor, the world will make a beaten

44

path to his door; no doubt about that; and in the gang that will trail along will be those who come, not to commend, but to condemn and to destroy his reputation. The late John H. Patterson, president of the National Cash Register Company, is a notable example of what may happen to a man who builds a better cash register than that of his neighbor; yet, in the mind of the accurate thinker, there is not one scintilla of evidence to support the vicious reports that Mr. Patterson's competitors circulated about him.

As for Wilson and Harding, we may only judge how posterity will view them by observing how it has immortalized the names of Lincoln and Washington. Truth, alone, endures. All else must pass on with Time.

The object of these references is not to eulogize those who stand in no particular need of eulogy; but, it is to direct your attention to the fact that "they say" evidence is always subject to the closest scrutiny; and all the more so when it is of a negative or destructive nature. No harm can come from accepting, as fact, hearsay evidence that is constructive; but its opposite, if accepted at all, should be subjected to the closest inspection possible under the available means of applying the law of evidence.

As an accurate thinker, it is both your privilege and your duty to avail yourself of facts, even though you must go out of your way to get them. If you permit yourself to be swayed to and fro by all manner of information that comes to your attention, you will never become an accurate thinker; and if you do not think accurately, you cannot be sure of attaining the object of your definite chief aim in life.

Many a man has gone down to defeat because, due to his prejudice and hatred, he underestimated the virtues of his enemies or competitors. The eyes of the accurate thinker see facts - not the delusions of prejudice, hate and envy.

An accurate thinker must be something of a good sportsman - in that he is fair enough (with himself at least) to look for virtues as well as faults in other people, for it is not without reason to suppose that all men have some of each of these qualities.

"I do not believe that I can afford to deceive others - I know I cannot afford to deceive myself!"

This must be the motto of the accurate thinker.

. . . .

With the supposition that these "hints" are sufficient to impress upon your mind the importance of searching for facts until you are reasonably sure that you have found them, we will take up the question of organizing, classifying and using these facts.

Look, once more, in the circle of your own acquaintances and find a person who appears to accomplish more with less effort than do any of his associates. Study this man and you observe that he is a strategist in that he has learned how to arrange facts so that he brings to his aid the Law of Increasing Returns which we described in a previous lesson.

The man who knows that he is working with facts goes at his task with a feeling of self-confidence which enables him to refrain from temporizing, hesitating or waiting to make sure of his ground. He knows in advance what the outcome of his efforts will be; therefore, he moves more rapidly and accomplishes more than does the man who must "feel his way" because he is not sure that he is working with facts.

The man who has learned of the advantages of searching for facts as the foundation of his thinking has gone a very long way toward the development of accurate thinking, but the man who has learned how to separate facts into the important and the unimportant has gone still further. The latter may be compared to the man who uses a trip-hammer, and thereby accomplishes at one blow more than the former, who uses a tack-hammer, can accomplish with ten thousand blows.

Let us analyze, briefly, a few men who have made it their business to deal with the important or relevant facts pertaining to their life-work.

If it were not for the fact that this course is being adapted to the practical needs of men and women of the present workaday world, we would go back to the great men of the past - Plato, Aristotle, Epictetus, Socrates, Solomon and Moses - and direct attention to their habit of dealing with facts. However, we can find examples nearer our own generation that will serve our purpose to better advantage at this particular point.

Inasmuch as this is an age in which money is looked upon as being the most concrete proof of success, let us study a man who has accumulatedalmost as much of it as has any other man in the history of the world - John D. Rockefeller.

Mr. Rockefeller has one quality that stands out, like a shining star, above all of his other qualities; it is his habit of dealing only with the relevant facts pertaining to his life-work. As a very young man (and a very poor young man, at that) Mr. Rockefeller adopted, as his definite chief aim, the accumulation of great wealth. It is not my purpose, nor is it of any particular advantage, to enter into Mr. Rockefeller's method of accumulating his fortune other than to observe that his most pronounced quality was that of insisting on facts as the basis of his business philosophy. Some there are who say that Mr. Rockefeller was not always fair with his competitors. That may or may not be true (as accurate thinkers we will leave the point undisturbed), but no one (not even his competitors) ever accused Mr. Rockefeller of forming "snap-judgments" or of underestimating the strength of his competitors. He not only recognized facts that affected his business, wherever and whenever he found them, but he made it his business to search for them until he was sure he had found them.

Thomas A. Edison is another example of a man who has attained to greatness through the organization, classification and use of relevant facts. Mr. Edison works with natural laws as his chief aids; therefore, he must be sure of his facts before he can harness those laws. Every time you press a button and switch on an electric light, remember that it was Mr. Edison's capacity for organizing relevant facts which made this possible.

Every time you hear a phonograph, remember thatMr. Edison is the man who made it a reality, through his persistent habit of dealing with relevant facts.

Every time you see a moving picture, remember that it was born of Mr. Edison's habit of dealing with important and relevant facts.

In the field of science relevant facts are the tools with which men and women work. Mere information, or hearsay evidence, is of no value to Mr. Edison; yet he might have wasted his life working with it, as millions of other people are doing.

Hearsay evidence could never have produced the incandescent electric light, the phonograph or the moving picture, and if it had, the phenomenon would have been an "accident." In this lesson we are trying to prepare the student to avoid "accidents."

The question now arises as to what constitutes an important and relevant fact.

The answer depends entirely upon what constitutes your definite chief aim in life, for an important and relevant fact is any fact which you can use, without interfering with the rights of others, in the attainment of that purpose.

All other facts, as far as you are concerned, are superfluous and of minor importance at most.

However, you can work just as hard in organizing, classifying and using unimportant and irrelevant facts as you can in dealing with their opposites, but you will not accomplish as much.

. . . .

Up to this point we have been discussing only one factor of accurate thought, that which is based upon deductive reasoning. Perhaps this is the point atwhich some of the students of this course will have to think along lines with which they are not familiar, for we come, now, to the discussion of thought which does much more than gather, organize and combine facts.

Let us call this creative thought!

That you may understand why it is called creative thought it is necessary briefly to study the process of evolution through which the thinking man has been created.

Thinking man has been a long time on the road of evolution, and he has traveled a very long way. In the words of judge T. Troward (in Bible Mystery and Bible Meaning), "Perfected man is the apex of the Evolutionary Pyramid, and this by a necessary sequence."

Let us trace thinking man through the five evolutionary steps through which we believe he has traveled, beginning with the very lowest; namely -

1. The Mineral Period. Here we find life in its lowest form, lying motionless and inert; a mass of mineral substances, with no power to move.

2. Then comes the Vegetable Period. Here we find life in a more active form, with intelligence sufficient to gather food, grow and reproduce, but still unable to move from its fixed moorings.

3. Then comes the Animal Period. Here we find life in a still higher and more intelligent form, with ability to move from place to place.

4. Then comes the Human or Thinking Man Period, where we find life in its highest known form; the highest, because man can think, and because thought is the highest known form of organized energy. In the realm of thought man knows no limitations. He can send his thoughts to the stars with the quickness of a flash of lightning. He can gather facts and assemble them in new and varying combinations. He can create hypotheses and translate them into physical reality, through thought. He can reason both inductively and deductively.

48

5. Then comes the Spiritual Period. On this plane the lower forms of life, described in the previously mentioned four periods, converge and become infinitude in nature. At this point thinking man has unfolded, expanded and grown until he has projected his thinking ability into infinite intelligence. As yet, thinking man is but an infant in this fifth period, for he has not learned how to appropriate to his own use this infinite intelligence called Spirit. Moreover, with a few rare exceptions, man has not yet recognized thought as the connecting link which gives him access to the power of infinite intelligence. These exceptions have been such men as Moses, Solomon, Plato, Aristotle, Socrates, Confucius and a comparatively small number of others of their type. Since their time we have had many who partly uncovered this great truth; yet the truth, itself, is as available now as it was then.

To make use of creative thought, one must work very largely on faith, which is the chief reason why more of us do not indulge in this sort of thought. The most ignorant of the race can think in terms of deductive reasoning, in connection with matters of a purely physical and material nature, but to go a step higher and think in terms of infinite intelligence is another question. The average man is totally at sea the moment he gets beyond that which he can comprehend with the aid of his five physical senses of seeing, hearing, feeling, smelling and tasting. Infinite intelligence works through none of these agencies and we cannot invoke its aid through any of them.

How, then, may one appropriate the power of infinite intelligence? is but a natural question.

And the answer is:

Through creative thought!

To make clear the exact manner in which this is done I will now call your attention to some of the preceding lessons of this course through which you have been prepared to understand the meaning of creative thought.

In the second lesson, and to some extent in practically every other lesson that followed it, up to this one, you have observed the frequent introduction of the term "Auto-suggestion." (Suggestion that you make to yourself.) We now come back to that term again, because Auto-suggestion is the telegraph line, so to speak, over which you may register in your subconscious mind a description or plan of that which you wish to create or acquire in physical form.

It is a process you can easily learn to use.

The sub-conscious mind is the intermediary between the conscious thinking mind and infinite intelligence, and you can invoke the aid of infinite intelligence only through the medium of the sub-conscious mind, by giving it clear instructions as to what you want. Here you become familiar with the psychological reason for a definite chief aim.

If you have not already seen the importance of creating a definite chief aim as the object of your life-work, you will undoubtedly do so before this lesson shall have been mastered.

Knowing, from my own experience as a beginner in the study of this and related subjects, how little I understood such terms as "Sub-conscious Mind" and "Auto-suggestion" and "Creative Thought," I have taken the liberty, throughout this course, of describing these terms through every conceivable simile and illustration, with the object of making their meaning and the method of their application so clear that no student of this course can possibly fail to understand. This accounts for the repetition of terms which you will observe throughout the course, and at the same time serves as an apology to those students who have already advanced far enough to grasp the meaning of much that the beginner will not understand at first reading.

The sub-conscious mind has one outstanding characteristic to which I will now direct your attention; namely, it records the suggestions which you send it through Auto-suggestion, and invokes the aid of infinite intelligence in translating these suggestions into their natural physical form, through natural means which are in no way out of the ordinary. If is important that you understand the foregoing sentence, for, if you fail to understand it, you are likely to fail, also, to understand the importance of the very foundation upon which this entire course is built - that foundation being the principle of infinite intelligence, which may be reached and appropriated at will through aid of the law of the "Master Mind" described in the Introductory Lesson. Study carefully, thoughtfully and with meditation, the entire preceding paragraph.

The sub-conscious mind has another outstanding characteristic - it accepts and acts upon all suggestions that reach it, whether they are constructive or destructive, and whether they come from the outside or from your own conscious mind.

You can see, therefore, how essential it is for you to observe the law of evidence and carefully follow the principles laid down in the beginning of this lesson, in the selection of that which you will pass on to your sub-conscious mind through Auto-suggestion. You can see why one must search diligently for facts, and why one cannot afford to lend a receptive ear to the slanderer and the scandalmonger - for to do so is the equivalent of feeding the sub-conscious mind with food that is poison and ruinous to creative thought.

The sub-conscious mind may be likened to the sensitive plate of a camera on which the picture of any object placed before the camera will be recorded. The plate of the camera does not choose the sort of picture to be recorded on it, it records anything which reaches it through the lens. The conscious mind may be likened to the shutter which shuts off the light from the sensitized plate, permitting nothing to reach the plate for record except that which the operator wishes to reach it. The lens of the camera may be likened to Auto-suggestion, for it is the medium which carries the image of the object to be registered, to the sensitized plate of the camera. And infinite intelligence may be likened to the one who develops the sensitized plate, after a picture has been recorded on it, thus bringing the picture into physical reality.

The ordinary camera is a splendid instrument with which to compare the whole process of creative thought. First comes the selection of the object to be exposed before the camera. This represents one's definite chief aim in life. Then comes the actual operation of recording a clear outline of that purpose, through the lens of Auto-suggestion, on the sensitized plate of the sub-conscious mind. Here infinite intelligence steps in and develops the outline of that purpose in a physical form appropriate to the nature of the purpose. The part which you must play is clear!

You select the picture to be recorded (definite chief aim). Then you fix your conscious mind upon this purpose with such intensity that it communicates with the sub-conscious mind, through Auto-suggestion, and registers that picture. You then begin to watch for and to expect manifestations of physical realization of the subject of that picture.

Bear in mind the fact that you do not sit down and wait, nor do you go to bed and sleep, with the expectation of awaking to find that infinite intelligence has showered you with the object of your definite chief aim. You go right ahead, in the usual way, doing your daily work in accordance with the instructions laid down in Lesson Nine of this course, with full faith and confidence that natural ways and means for the attainment of the object of your definite purpose will open to you at the proper time and in a suitable manner.

The way may not open suddenly, from the first step to the last, but it may open one step at a time. Therefore, when you are conscious of an opportunity to take the first step, take it without hesitation, and do the same when the second, and the third, and all subsequent steps, essential for the attainment of the object of your definite chief aim, are manifested to you.

Infinite intelligence will not build you a home and deliver that home to you, ready to enter; but infinite intelligence will open the way and provide the necessary means with which you may build your own house.

Infinite intelligence will not command the cashier of your bank to place a definite sum of money to your credit, just because you suggested this to your subconscious mind; but infinite intelligence will open to you the way in which you may earn or borrow that money and place it to your own credit.

Infinite intelligence will not throw out the present incumbent of the White House and make you President in his place; but infinite intelligence would most likely proceed, under the proper circumstances, to influence you to prepare yourself to fill that position with credit and then help you to attain it through the regular method of procedure.

Do not rely upon the performance of miracles for the attainment of the object of your definite chief aim; rely upon the power of infinite intelligence to guide you, through natural channels, and with the aid of natural laws, for its attainment. Do not expect infinite intelligence to bring to you the object of your definite chief aim; instead, expect infinite intelligence to direct you toward that object.

As a beginner, do not expect infinite intelligence to move quickly in your behalf; but, as you becomemore adept in the use of the principle of Auto-suggestion, and as you develop the faith and understanding required for its quick realization, you can create a definite chief aim and witness its immediate translation into physical reality. You did not walk the first time you tried, but now, as an adult (an adept at walking), you walk without effort. You also look down at the little child as it wobbles around, trying to walk, and laugh at its efforts. As a beginner in the use of creative thought, you may be compared to the little child who is learning to take its first step.

I have the best of reasons for knowing that this comparison is accurate, but I will not state them. I will let you find out your own reason, in your own way.

Keep in mind, always, the principle of evolution through the operation of which everything physical is eternally reaching upward and trying to complete the cycle between finite and infinite intelligences.

Man, himself, is the highest and most noteworthy example of the working of the principle of evolution. First, we find him down in the minerals of the earth, where there is life but no intelligence. Next, we find him raised, through the growth of vegetation (evolution), to a much higher form of life, where he enjoys sufficient intelligence to feed himself. Next, we find him functioning in the animal period, where he has a comparatively high degree of intelligence, with ability to move around from place to place. Lastly, we find him risen above the lower species of the animal kingdom, to where he functions as a thinking entity, with ability to appropriate and use infinite intelligence.

Observe that he did not reach this high state all at one bound. He climbed - step by step, perhaps through many reincarnations. Keep this in mind and you will understand why you cannot reasonably expect infinite intelligence to circumvent the natural laws and turn man into the storehouse of all knowledge and all power until he has prepared himself to use this knowledge and power with higher than finite intelligence.

If you want a fair example of what may happen to a man who suddenly comes into control of power, study some newly-rich or someone who has inherited a fortune. Money-power in the hands of John D. Rockefeller is not only in safe hands, but it is in hands where it is serving mankind throughout the world, blotting out ignorance, destroying contagious disease and serving in a thousand other ways of which the average individual knows nothing.

But place John D. Rockefeller's fortune in the hands of some young lad who has not yet finished high school and you might have another story to tell, the details of which your own imagination and your knowledge of human nature will supply.

I will have more to say on this subject in Lesson Fourteen.

If you have ever done any farming, you understand that certain preparations are necessary before a crop can be produced from the ground. You know, of course, that grain will not grow in the woods, that it requires sunshine and rain for its growth. Likewise, you understand that the farmer must plow the soil and properly plant the grain.

After all this has been done, he then waits onNature to do her share of the work; and she does it in due time, without outside help.

This is a perfect simile which illustrates the method through which one may attain the object of one's definite chief aim. First comes the preparing of the soil to receive the seed, which is represented by faith and infinite intelligence and understanding of the principle of Auto-suggestion and the sub-conscious mind through which the seed of a definite purpose may be planted. Then comes a period of waiting and working for the realization of the object of that purpose. During this period, there must be continuous, intensified faith, which serves as the sunshine and the rain, without which the seed will wither and die in the ground. Then comes realization, harvest-time.

And a wonderful harvest can be brought forth.

I am fully conscious of the fact that much of that which I am stating will not be understood by the beginner, at the first reading, for I have in mind my own experiences at the start. However, as the evolutionary process carries on its work (and it will do so; make no mistake about this) all the principles described in this and in all other lessons of this course, will become as familiar to you as did the multiplication table after you had mastered it; and, what is of greater importance still, these principles will work with the same unvarying certainty as does the principle of multiplication.

Each lesson of this course has provided you with definite instructions to follow. The instructions have been simplified as far as possible, so anyone can understand them. Nothing has been left to the student except to follow the instructions and supply the faithin their soundness without which they would be useless.

In this lesson you are dealing with four major factors to which I would again direct your attention with the request that you familiarize yourself with them. They are:

Auto-suggestion, the Sub-conscious Mind, Creative Thought and Infinite Intelligence.

These are the four roadways over which you must travel in your upward climb in quest of knowledge. Observe that you control three of these. Observe, also - and this is especially emphasized - that upon the manner in which you traverse these three roadways will depend the time and place at which they will converge into the fourth, or infinite intelligence.

You understand what is meant by the terms Autosuggestion and Sub-conscious Mind. Let us make sure that you understand, also, what is meant by the term Creative Thought. This means thought of a positive, non-destructive, creative nature. The object of Lesson Eight, on Self-control, was to prepare you to understand and successfully apply the principle of Creative Thought. If you have not mastered that lesson you are not ready to make use of Creative Thought in the attainment of your definite chief aim.

Let me repeat a simile already used by saying that your sub-conscious mind is the field or the soil in which you sow the seed of your definite chief aim. Creative Thought is the instrument with which you keep that soil fertilized and conditioned to awaken that seed into growth and maturity. Your subconscious mind will not germinate the seed of your definite chief aim nor will infinite intelligence translate that purpose into physical reality if you fill your mind with hatred, and envy, and jealousy, and selfishness and greed. These negative or destructive thoughts are the weeds which will choke out the seed of your definite purpose.

Creative thought pre-supposes that you will keep your mind in a state of expectancy of attainment of the object of your definite chief aim; that you will have full faith and confidence in its attainment in due course and in due order.

If this lesson does that which it was intended to do, it will bring you a fuller and deeper realization of the third lesson of this course, on Self-confidence. As you begin to learn how to plant the seed of your desires in the fertile soil of your sub-conscious mind, and how to fertilize that seed until it springs into life and action, you will then have reason, indeed, to believe in yourself.

And, after you have reached this point in the process of your evolution, you will have sufficient knowledge of the real source from which you are drawing your power, to give full credit to infinite intelligence for all that you had previously credited to your Self-confidence.

. . . .

Auto-suggestion is a powerful weapon with which one may rise to heights of great achievement, when it is used constructively. Used in a negative manner, however, it may destroy all possibility of success, and if so used continuously it will actually destroy health. Careful comparison of the experiences of leading physicians and psychiatrists disclosed the startling in-formation that approximately seventy-five per cent of those who are ill are suffering from hypochondria, which is a morbid state of mind causing useless anxiety about one's health.

Stated in plain language, the hypochondriac is a person who believes he or she is suffering with some sort of imaginary disease, and often these unfortunates believe they have every disease of which they ever heard the name.

Hypochondriacal conditions are generally super-induced by auto-intoxication, or poisoning through failure of the intestinal system to throw off the waste matter. The person who suffers with such a toxic condition is not only unable to think with accuracy, but suffers from all sorts of perverted, destructive, illusory thoughts. Many sick people have tonsils removed, or teeth pulled, or the appendix taken out, when their trouble could have been removed with an internal bath and a bottle of Citrate of Magnesia (with due apologies to my friends, the physicians, one of the leading of whom gave me this information).

Hypochondria is the beginning of most cases of insanity!

Dr. Henry R. Rose is authority for the following typical example of the power of Auto-suggestion:

"'If my wife dies I will not believe there is a God' His wife was ill with pneumonia, and this is the way he greeted me when I reached his home. She had sent for me because the doctor had told her she could not recover. (Most doctors know better than to make a statement such as this in the presence of a patient.) She had called her husband and two sons to her bedside and bidden them good-by. Then she asked thatI, her minister, be sent for. I found the husband in the front room sobbing and the sons doing their best to brace her up. When I went into her room she was breathing with difficulty, and the trained nurse told me she was very low.

"I soon found that Mrs. N_ had sent for me to look after her two sons after she was gone. Then I said to her: 'You mustn't give up. YOU ARE NOT GOING TO DIE! You have always been a strong and healthy woman and I do not believe God wants you to die and leave your boys to me or anyone else.'

"I talked to her along this line and then read the 103d Psalm and made a prayer in which I prepared her to get well rather than to enter eternity. I told her to put her faith in God and throw her mind and will against every thought of dying. Then I left her, saying, 'I will come again, and I will then find you much better.'

"This was on Sunday morning. I called that afternoon. Her husband met me with a smile. He said that the moment I had gone his wife called him and the boys into the room and said: 'Dr. Rose says that I am not going to die; that I am going to get well, and I am.'

"She did get well. But what did it? Two things Auto-suggestion, superinduced by the suggestion I had given her, and faith on her part. I came just in the nick of time, and so great was her faith in me that I was able to inspire faith in herself. It was that faith that tipped the scales and brought her through the pneumonia. No medicine can cure pneumonia. The physicians admit that. There are cases of pneumonia, perhaps, that nothing can cure. We all sadly agree tothat, but there are times, as in this case, when the mind, if worked upon and worked with in just the right way, will turn the tide. While there is life there is hope; but hope must rule supreme and do the good that hope was intended to do.

"Here is another remarkable case showing the power of the human mind when used constructively. A physician asked me to see Mrs. H_. He said there was nothing organically wrong with her, but she just wouldn't eat. Having made up her mind that she could not retain anything on her stomach, she had quit eating, and was slowly starving herself to death. I went to see her and found, first, that she had no religious belief. She had lost her faith in God. I also found that she had no confidence in her power to retain food. My first effort was to restore her faith in the Almighty and to get her to believe that He was with her and would give her power. Then I told her that she could eat anything she wanted. True, her confidence in me was great and my statement impressed her. She began to eat from that day! She was out of her bed in three days, for the first time in weeks. She is a normal, healthy and happy woman today.

"What did it? The same forces as those described in the preceding case; outside suggestion (which she accepted in faith and applied, through self-suggestion) and inward confidence.

"There are times when the mind is sick and it makes the body sick. At such times it needs a stronger mind to heal it by giving it direction and especially by giving it confidence and faith in itself. This is called suggestion. It is transmitting your confidence andpower to another, and with such force as to make the other believe as you wish and do as you will. It need not be hypnotism. You can get wonderful results with the patient wide awake and perfectly rational. The patient must believe in you and you must understand the workings of the human mind in order to meet the arguments and questions of the patient. Each one of us can be a healer of this sort and thus help our fellow men.

"It is the duty of every person to read some of the best books on the forces of the human mind and learn what amazing things the mind can do to keep people well and happy. We see the terrible things that wrong thinking does to people, even going to such lengths as to make them positively insane. It is high time we found out the good things the mind can do, not only to cure mental disorders, but physical diseases as well"

You should delve deeper into this subject.

I do not say the mind can cure everything. There is no reliable evidence that certain forms of cancer have been cured by thinking or faith or any mental or religious process. If you would be cured of cancer you must take it at the very beginning and treat it surgically. There is no other way, and it would be criminal to suggest that there is. But the mind can do much with so many types of human indisposition and disease that we ought to rely upon it more often than we do.

Napoleon, during his campaign in Egypt, went among his soldiers who were dying by the hundreds of the black plague. He touched one of them and lifted a second, to inspire the others not to be afraid, for the awful disease seemed to spread as much by the aid of the imagination as in any other way. Goethe tells us that he himself went where there was malignant fever and never contracted it because he put forth his will. These giants among men knew something WE ARE SLOWLY BEGINNING TO FIND OUT - the power of Auto-suggestion! This means the influence we have upon ourselves by believing we cannot catch a disease or be sick. There is something about the operation of the automatic or sub-conscious mind by which it rises above disease germs and bids defiance to them when we resolve not to let the thought of them frighten us, or when we go in and out among the sick, even the contagiously sick, without thinking anything about it.

"Imagination will kill a cat," so runs the old adage. It certainly will kill a man, or, on the other hand, it will help him rise to heights of achievement of the most astounding nature, providing he uses it as the basis of self-confidence. There are authentic cases on record of men having actually died because they imagined they were cut by a knife across the jugular vein, when in reality a piece of ice was used and water was allowed to drip so they could hear it and imagine their blood was running out. They had been blindfolded before the experiment was begun. No matter how well you may be when you start for work in the morning, if everyone you meet should say to you, "How ill you look; you should see a doctor," it will not be long before you begin to feel ill, and if this keeps up a few hours you will arrive at home in the evening as limp as a rag and ready for a doctor. Such is the power of the imagination or Auto-suggestion.

The imaginative faculty of the human mind is a marvelous piece of mental machinery, but it may, and usually does, play queer tricks on us unless we keep constantly on guard and control it.

If you allow your imagination to "expect the worst" it will play havoc with you. Young medical students not infrequently become frightened and believe they have every disease on the medical calendar, as the result of medical lectures and class-room discussions of the various diseases.

As has been stated, hypochondria may often be superinduced by toxic poisoning, through improper elimination of the waste matter of the body; also, it may be brought on by false alarm, through improper use of the imagination. In other words, the hypochondriacal condition may have as its cause a real physical basis, or it may arise entirely as the result of allowing the imagination to run wild.

Physicians are pretty well agreed upon this point!

Dr. Schofield describes the case of a woman who had a tumor. They placed her on the operating table and gave her anesthetics, when lo! the tumor immediately disappeared, and no operation was necessary. But when she came back to consciousness the tumor returned. The physician then learned that she had been living with a relative who had a real tumor, and that her imagination was so vivid that she had imagined this one upon herself. She was placed on the operating table again, given anesthetics and then she was strapped around the middle so that the tumor could not artificially return. When she revived she was told that a successful operation had been performed but that it would be necessary to wear thebandage for several days. She believed the doctor, and when the bandage was finally removed the tumor did not return. No operation whatever had been performed. She had simply relieved her sub-conscious mind of the thought that she had a tumor and her imagination had nothing to work upon save the idea of health, and, as she had never really been sick, of course she remained normal.

The mind may be cured of imaginary ills in exactly the same manner that it became diseased with those ills, by Auto-suggestion. The best time to work on a faulty imagination is at night, just as you are ready to go to sleep, for then the automatic or sub-conscious mind has everything its own way, and the thoughts or suggestions you give it just as your conscious or "day" mind is about to go off duty will be taken up and worked on during the night.

This may seem impossible, but you can easily test the principle by the following procedure: You wish to get up at seven o'clock tomorrow morning, or at some hour other than your regular time to awaken. Say to yourself, as you are about ready to go to sleep, "I must arise at seven o'clock tomorrow without fail." Repeat this several times, at the same time impressing the fact upon your mind that you must actually arise at the precise moment mentioned. Turn this thought over to your sub-conscious mind with absolute confidence that you will awaken at seven o'clock, and when that hour arrives your sub-conscious mind will awaken you. This test has been successfully made hundreds of times. The sub-conscious mind will awaken you, at any hour you demand, just as if someone came to your bed and tapped you on the shoulder. But you mustgive the command in no uncertain or indefinite terms.

Likewise, the sub-conscious mind may be given any other sort of orders and it will carry them out as readily as it will awaken you at a given hour. For example, give the command, as you are about to go to sleep each night, for your sub-conscious mind to develop self-confidence, courage, initiative or any other quality, and it will do your bidding.

If the imagination of man can create imaginary ills and send one to bed with those ills, it can also, and just as easily, remove the cause of those ills.

· · · · · · · ·

60

Man is a combination of chemical equivalents the value of which is said to be about twenty-six dollars, with the exception, of course, of that stupendous power called the human mind.

In the aggregate the mind seems to be a complicated machine, but in reality; as far as the manner in which it may be used is concerned, it is the nearest thing to perpetual motion that is known. It works automatically when we are asleep; it works both automatically and in conjunction with the will, or voluntary section, when we are awake.

The mind is deserving of the minutest possible analysis in this lesson because the mind is the energy with which all thinking is done. To learn how to THINK ACCURATELY, the teaching of which is the sole object of this lesson, one must thoroughly understand:

First: That the mind can be controlled, guided and directed to creative, constructive ends.

Second: That the mind can be directed to destructive ends, and, that it may, voluntarily, tear down and destroy unless it is with plan and deliberation controlled and directed constructively.

Third: That the mind has power over every cell of the body, and can be made to cause every cell to do its intended work perfectly, or it may, through neglect or wrong direction, destroy the normal functionary purposes of any or all cells.

Fourth: That all achievement of man is the result of thought, the part which his physical body plays being of secondary importance, and in many instances of no importance whatsoever except as a housing place for the mind.

Fifth: That the greatest of all achievements, whether in literature, art, finance, industry, commerce, transportation, religion, politics or scientific discoveries, are usually the results of ideas conceived in one man's brain but ACTUALLY TRANSFORMED INTO REALITY BY OTHER MEN, through the combined use of their minds and bodies. (Meaning that the conception of an idea is of greater importance than the transformation of that idea into more material form, because relatively few men can conceive useful ideas, while there are hundreds of millions who can develop an idea and give it material form after it has been conceived.)

Sixth: The majority of all thoughts conceived in the minds of men are not ACCURATE, being more in the nature of "opinions" or "snap-judgments."

When Alexander the Great sighed because he had no more worlds (as he believed) that could be conquered he was in a frame of mind similar to that of the present-day "Alexanders" of science, industry, invention, etc., whose "accurate thoughts" have conquered the air and the sea, explored practically every square mile of the little earth on which we live, and wrested from Nature thousands of "secrets" which, a few generations ago, would have been set down as "miracles" of the most astounding and imponderable sort.

In all this discovery and mastery of mere physical substances is it not strange, indeed, that we have practically neglected and overlooked the most marvelous of all powers, the human mind! All scientific men who have made a study of the human mind readily agree on this - that the surface has not yet been scratched in the study of the wonderful power which lies dormant in the mind of man, waiting, as the oak tree sleeps in the acorn, to be aroused and put to work. Those who have expressed themselves on the subject are of the opinion that the next great cycle of discovery lies in the realm of the human mind.

The possible nature of these discoveries has been suggested, in many different ways, in practically every lesson of this course, particularly in this and the following lessons of the course.

If these suggestions appear to lead the student of this philosophy into deeper water than he or she is accustomed to, bear in mind the fact that the student has the privilege of stopping at any depth desired, until ready, through thought and study, to go further.

The author of this course has found it necessary to take the lead, and to keep far enough ahead, as it were, to induce the student to go at least a few paces ahead of the normal average range of human thought.It is not expected that any beginner will, at first, try to assimilate and put into use all that has been included in this philosophy. But, if the net result of the course is nothing more than to sow the seed of constructive thought in the mind of the student the author's work will have been completed. Time, plus the student's own desire for knowledge, will do the rest.

This is an appropriate place to state frankly that many of the suggestions passed on through this course would, if literally followed, lead the student far beyond the necessary bounds and present needs of what is ordinarily called business philosophy. Stated differently, this course goes more deeply into the functioning processes of the human mind than is necessary as far as the use of this philosophy as a means of achieving business or financial success is concerned.

However, it is presumed that many students of this course will wish to go more deeply into the study of mind power than may be required for purely material achievement, and the author has had in mind these students throughout the labor of organizing and writing this course.

SUMMARY OF PRINCIPLES INVOLVED IN ACCURATE THINKING

We have discovered that the body of man is not singular, but plural - that it consists of billions on top of billions of living, intelligent, individual cells which carry on a very definite, well organized work of building, developing and maintaining the human body.

We have discovered that these cells are directed, in their respective duties, by the sub-conscious orautomatic action of the mind; that the subconscious section of the mind can be, to a very large extent, controlled and directed by the conscious or voluntary section of the mind.

We have found that any idea or thought which is held in the mind, through repetition, has a tendency to direct the physical body to transform such thought or idea into its material equivalent. We have found that any order that is PROPERLY given to the subconscious section of the mind (through the law of Auto-suggestion) will be carried out unless it is sidetracked or countermanded by another and stronger order. We have found that the sub-conscious mind does not question the source from which it receives orders, nor the soundness of those orders, but it will proceed to direct the muscular system of the body to carry out any order it receives.

This explains the necessity for guarding closely the environment from which we receive suggestions, and by which we are subtly and quietly influenced at times and in ways of which we do not take cognizance through the conscious mind.

We have found that every movement of the human body is controlled by either the conscious or the subconscious section of the mind; that not a muscle can be moved until an order has been sent out by one or the other of these two sections of the mind, for the movement.

When this principle is thoroughly understood we understand, also, the powerful effect of any idea or thought which we create through the faculty of IMAGINATION and hold in the conscious mind until the sub-conscious section of the mind has time to takeover that thought and begin the work of transforming it into its material counterpart. When we understand the principle through which any idea is first placed in the conscious mind, and held there until the subconscious section of the mind picks it up and appropriates it, we have a practical working knowledge of the Law of Concentration, covered by next lesson (and, it might be added, we have also a thorough understanding of the reason why the Law of Concentration is necessarily a part of this philosophy). When we understand this working relationship between the imagination, the conscious mind and the sub-conscious section of the mind, we can see that the very first step in the achievement of any definite chief aim is to create a definite picture of that which is desired. This picture is then placed in the conscious mind, through the Law of Concentration, and held there (through the formulas described in next lesson) until the sub-conscious section of the mind picks it up and translates it into its ultimate and desired form.

Surely this principle has been made clear. It has been stated and restated, over and over, not only for the purpose of thoroughly describing it, but, of greater importance, to IMPRESS UPON THE MIND OF THE STUDENT THE PART IT PLAYS IN ALL HUMAN ACHIEVEMENT.

THE VALUE OF ADOPTING A CHIEF AIM

This lesson on Accurate Thought not only describes the real purpose of a definite chief aim, but it explains in simple terms the principles through which such an aim or purpose may be realized. Wefirst create the objective toward which we are striving, through the imaginative faculty of the mind, then transfer an outline of this objective to paper by writing out a definite statement of it in the nature of a definite chief aim. By daily reference to this written statement the idea or thing aimed for is taken up by the conscious mind and handed over to the sub-conscious mind, which, in turn, directs the energies of the body to transform the desire into material form.

DESIRE

Strong, deeply rooted desire is the starting point of all achievement. Just as the electron is the last unit of matter discernible to the scientist, DESIRE is the seed of all achievement; the starting place, back of which there is nothing, or at least there is nothing of which we have any knowledge.
A definite chief aim, which is only another name for DESIRE, would be meaningless unless based upon a deeply seated, strong desire for the object of the chief aim. Many people "wish" for many things, but a wish is not the equivalent of a strong DESIRE, and therefore wishes are of little or no value unless they are crystallized into the more definite form of DESIRE.
It is believed by men who have devoted years of research to the subject, that all energy and matter throughout the universe respond to and are controlled by the Law of Attraction which causes elements and forces of a similar nature to gather around certain centers of attraction. It is through the operation of this same universal Law of Attraction that constant, deeply seated, strong DESIRE attracts the physical equivalent or counterpart of the thing desired, or the means of securing it.
We have learned, then, if this hypothesis is correct, that all cycles of human achievement work somewhat after this fashion: First, we picture in our conscious minds, through a definite chief aim (based upon a strong desire), some objective; we then focus our conscious mind upon this objective, by constant thought of it and belief in its attainment, until the subconscious section of the mind takes up the picture or outline of this objective and impels us to take the necessary physical action to transform that picture into reality.

SUGGESTION AND AUTO-SUGGESTION

Through this and other lessons of the Law of Success course the student has learned that sense impressions arising out of one's environment, or from statements or actions of other people, are called suggestions, while sense impressions that we place in our own minds are placed there by self-suggestion, or Autosuggestion. All suggestions coming from others, or from environment, influence us only after we have accepted them and passed them on to the sub-conscious mind, through the principle of Auto-suggestion, thus it is seen that suggestion becomes, and must become, Autosuggestion before it influences the mind of the one receiving it.

Stated in another way, no one may influence another without the consent of the one influenced, asthe influencing is done through one's own power of Auto-suggestion.

The conscious mind stands, during the hours when one is awake, as a sentinel, guarding the sub-conscious mind and warding off all suggestions which try to reach it from the outside, until those suggestions have been examined by the conscious mind, passed upon and accepted. This is Nature's way of safeguarding the human being against intruders who would otherwise take control of any mind desired at will.

It is a wise arrangement.

THE VALUE OF AUTO-SUGGESTION IN AC-COMPLISHING THE OBJECT OF YOUR
DEFINITE CHIEF AIM

One of the greatest uses to which one may direct the power of Auto-suggestion is that of making it help accomplish the object of one's definite chief aim in life.

The procedure through which this may be accomplished is very simple. While the exact formula has been stated in Lesson Two, and referred to in many other lessons of the course, the principle upon which it is based will be here, again, described, viz.:

Write out a clear, concise statement of that which you intend to accomplish, as your definite chief aim, covering a period of, let us say, the next five years. Make at least two copies of your statement, one to be placed where you can read it several times a day, while you are at work, and the other to be placed in the room where you sleep, where it can be read several times each evening before you go to sleep and just after you arise in the morning.

The suggestive influence of this procedure (im-practical though it may seem) will soon impress the object of your definite chief aim on your sub-conscious mind and, as if by a stroke of magic, you will begin to observe events taking place which will lead you nearer and nearer the attainment of that object.

From the very day that you reach a definite decision in your own mind as to the precise thing, condition or position in life that you deeply desire, you will observe, if you read books, newspapers and magazines, that important news items and other data bearing on the object of your definite chief aim will begin to come to your attention; you will observe, also, that opportunities will begin to come to you that will, if embraced, lead you nearer and nearer the coveted goal of your desire. No one knows better than the author of this course how impossible and impractical this may seem to the person who is not informed on the subject of mind operation; however, this is not an age favorable to the doubter or the skeptic, and the best thing for any person to do is to experiment with this principle until its practicality has been established.

To the present generation it may seem that there are no more worlds to conquer in the field of mechanical invention, but every thinker (even those who are not accurate thinkers) will concede that we are just entering a new era of evolution, experiment and analysis as far as the powers of the human mind are concerned. The word "impossible" means less now than ever before in the history of the human race. There are some who have actually removed this word from their vocabularies, believing that man can do anything he can imagine and BELIEVE HE CAN DO!

We have learned, for sure, that the universe is made up of two substances: matter and energy. Through patient scientific research we have discovered what we believe to be good evidence that everything that is or ever has been in the way of matter, when analyzed to the finest point, can be traced back to the electron, which is nothing but a form of energy. On the other hand, every material thing that man has created began in the form of energy, through the seed of an idea that was released through the imaginative faculty of the human mind. In other words, the beginning of every material thing is energy and the ending of it is energy.

All matter obeys the command of one form or another of energy. The highest known form of energy is that which functions as the human mind. The human mind, therefore, is the sole directing force of everything man creates, and what he may create with: this force in the future, as compared with that which he has created with it in the past, will make his past achievements seem petty and small.

We do not have to wait for future discoveries in connection with the powers of the human mind for evidence that the mind is the greatest force known to mankind. We know, now, that any idea, aim or purpose that is fixed in the mind and held there with a will to achieve or attain its physical or material equivalent, puts into motion powers that cannot be conquered.

Buxton said: "The longer I live the more certain I am that the great difference between men, between the feeble and the powerful, the great and the insignificant, is energy - invincible determination - apurpose once fixed, and then death or victory. That quality will do anything that can be done in this world - and no talents, no circumstances, no opportunities will make a two-legged creature a man without it."

Donald G. Mitchell has well said: "Resolve is what makes a man manifest. Not puny resolve; not crude determinations; not errant purposes - but that strong and indefatigable will which treads down difficulties and danger, as a boy treads down the heaving frost-lands of winter, which kindles his eye and brain with proud pulse beat toward the unattainable. WILL MAKES MEN GIANTS!"

The great Disraeli said: "I have brought myself, by long meditation, to the conviction that a human being with a settled purpose must accomplish it, and that nothing can resist a will which will stake even existence upon its fulfillment."

Sir John Simpson said: "A passionate DESIRE and an unwearied will can perform impossibilities, or what may seem to be such to the cold, timid and feeble."

And John Foster adds his testimony when he says: "It is wonderful how even the casualties of life seem to bow to a spirit that will not bow to them, and yield to subserve a design which they may, in their first apparent tendency, threaten to frustrate. When a firm, decisive spirit is recognized, it is curious to see how the space clears around a man and leaves him room and freedom."

Abraham Lincoln said of General Grant: "The great thing about Grant is his cool persistency of purpose. He is not easily excited, and he has got the grip of a bull-dog. When he once gets his teeth in, nothing can shake him off."

It seems appropriate to state here that a strong desire, to be transformed into reality, must be backed with persistency until it is taken over by the subconscious mind. It is not enough to feel very deeply the desire for achievement of a definite chief aim, for a few hours or a few days, and then forget all about that desire. The desire must be placed in the mind and held there, with PERSISTENCE THAT KNOWS NO DEFEAT, until the automatic or sub-conscious mind takes it over. Up to this point you must stand back of the desire and push it; beyond this point the desire will stand back of you and push you on to achievement.

Persistence may be compared to the dropping of water which finally wears away the hardest stone. When the final chapter of your life shall have been completed it will be found that your persistence, or lack of this sterling quality, played an important part in either your success or your failure.

This author watched the Tunney-Dempsey fight, in Chicago. He also studied the psychology leading up to and surrounding their previous bout. Two things helped Tunney defeat Dempsey, on both occasions, despite the fact that Dempsey is the stronger of the two men, and, as many believe, the better fighter.

And these two things, which spelled Dempsey's doom, were, first, his own lack of self-confidence - the fear that Tunney might defeat him; and, second, Tunny's complete self-reliance and his belief that he would whip Dempsey.

Tunney stepped into the ring, with his chin in theair, an atmosphere of self-assurance and certainty written in his every movement. Dempsey walked in, with a sort of uncertain stride, eying Tunney in a manner that plainly queried, "I wonder what you'll do to me?"

Dempsey was whipped, in his own mind, before he entered the ring. Press agents and propagandists had done the trick, thanks to the superior thinking ability of his opponent, Tunney.

And so the story goes, from the lowest and most brutal of occupations, prize-fighting, on up to the highest and most commendable professions. Success is won by the man who understands how to use his power of thought.

Throughout this course much stress has been laid upon the importance of environment and habit out of which grow the stimuli that put the "wheels" of the human mind into operation.

Fortunate is the person who has found how to arouse or stimulate his or her mind so that the powers of that mind will function constructively, as they may be made to do when placed back of any strong, deeply seated desire.

Accurate thinking is thinking that makes intelligent use of all the powers of the human mind, and does not stop with the mere examination, classification and arranging of ideas. Accurate thought creates ideas and it may be made to transform these ideas into their most profitable, constructive form.

· · · · · · · ·

The student will perhaps be better prepared to analyze, without a feeling of skepticism and doubt, the principles laid down in this lesson if the fact is kept in mind that the conclusions and hypotheses here enumerated are not solely those of the author. I have had the benefit of close co-operation from some of the leading investigators in the field of mental phenomena, and conclusions reached, as stated in this entire course, are those of many different minds.

. . . .

In the lesson on Concentration, you will be further instructed in the method of applying the principle of Auto-suggestion. In fact, throughout the course, the principle of gradual unfoldment has been followed, paralleling that of the principle of evolution as nearly as possible. The first lesson laid the foundation for the second, and the second prepared the way for the third, and so on. I have tried to build this course just as Nature builds a man - by a series of steps each of which lifts the student just another step higher and nearer the apex of the pyramid which the course, as a whole, represents.

The purpose in building this course in the manner outlined is one that cannot be described in words, but that purpose will become obvious and clear to you as soon as you shall have mastered the course, for its mastery will open to you a source of knowledge which cannot be imparted by one man to another, but is attainable only by educing, drawing out and expanding, from within one's own mind. The reason this knowledge cannot be imparted by one to another is the same as that which makes it impossible for one person to describe colors to a blind person who has never seen colors.

The knowledge of which I write became obviousto me only after I had diligently and faithfully followed the instructions which I have laid down in this course for your guidance and enlightenment; therefore, I speak from experience when I say that there are no illustrations, similes or words with which to describe this knowledge adequately. It can only be imparted from within.

With this vague "hint" as to the reward which awaits all who earnestly and intelligently search for the hidden passageway to knowledge to which I refer, we will now discuss that phase of accurate thought which will take you as high as you can go-except through the discovery and use of the secret passageway to which I have alluded.

Thoughts are things!

It is the belief of many that every completed thought starts an unending vibration with which the one who releases it will have to contend at a later time; that man, himself, is but the physical reflection of thought that was put into motion by infinite intelligence.

"And the Word was made flesh, and dwelt among us, (and we beheld his glory, the glory as of the only begotten of the Father,) full of grace and truth." (St. John i, 13.)

The only hope held out to mankind in the entire Bible is of a reward which may be attained in no way except by constructive thought. This is a startling statement, but if you are even an elementary student and interpreter of the Bible you understand that it is a true statement.

If the Bible is plain on any one point above all others, it is on the fact that thought is the beginning of all things of a material nature. At the beginning of every lesson of this course you will observe this motto:

"You can do it if you BELIEVE you can!"

This sentence is based upon a great truth which is practically the major premise of the entire Bible teaching. Observe the emphasis which is placed upon the word BELIEVE. Back of this word "believe" lies the power with which you can vitalize and give life to the suggestions that you pass on to your sub-conscious mind, through the principle of Auto-suggestion, with the aid of the law of the Master Mind. Do not miss this point. You cannot afford to miss it, as it is the very beginning, the middle and the end of all the power you will ever have.

All thought is creative! However, not all thought is constructive or positive. If you think thoughts of misery and poverty and see no way to avoid these conditions, then your thoughts will create those very conditions and curse you with them. But reverse the order, and think thoughts of a positive, expectant nature and your thoughts will create those conditions.

Thought magnetizes your entire personality and attracts to you the outward, physical things that harmonize with the nature of your thoughts. This has been made clear in practically every lesson preceding this one, yet it is repeated here, and will be repeated many times more in the lessons that follow. The reason for this constant repetition is that nearly all beginners in the study of mind operation overlook the importance of this fundamental and eternal truth.

When you plant a definite chief aim in your subconscious mind you must fertilize it with full belief that infinite intelligence will step in and mature that purpose into reality in exact accordance with the nature of the purpose. Anything short of such belief will bring you disappointment.

When you suggest a definite chief aim which embodies some definite desire, in your sub-conscious mind, you must accompany it with such faith and belief in the ultimate realization of that purpose that you can actually see yourself in possession of the object of the purpose. Conduct yourself in the exact manner in which you would if you were already in possession of the object of your definite purpose, from the moment you suggest it to your sub-conscious mind.

Do not question; do not wonder if the principles of Auto-suggestion will work; do not doubt, but believe!

Surely this point has been sufficiently emphasized to impress upon your mind its importance. Positive belief in the attainment of your definite purpose is the very germ with which you fertilize the "egg of your thought" and if you fail to give it this fertilization, you might as well expect an unfertilized hen-egg to produce a chicken as to expect the attainment of the object of your definite chief aim.

You never can tell what a thought will do
In bringing you hate or love;
For thoughts are things, and their airy wings
Are swifter than a carrier dove.
They follow the law of the universe, -
Each thought creates its kind,
And they speed o'er the track to bring you back
Whatever went out from your mind.

Thoughts are things! This is a great truth which, when you understand it, will bring you as close to the door of that secret passage-way to knowledge, previously mentioned, as is possible for another person to bring you. When you grasp this fundamental truth you will soon find that door and open it.

The power to think as you wish to think is the only power over which you have absolute control.

Please read and study the foregoing sentence until you grasp its meaning. If it is within your power to control your thoughts the responsibility then rests upon you as to whether your thoughts will be of the positive or the negative type, which brings to mind one of the world's most famous poems:

Out of the night that covers me,
Black as the pit from pole to pole,
I thank whatever gods may be
For my unconquerable soul.

In the fell clutch of circumstance
I have not winced or cried aloud.
Under the bludgeonings of chance
My head is bloody, but unbowed.

Beyond this place of wrath and tears
Looms but the horror of the shade,
And yet the menace of the years
Finds, and shall find, me unafraid.

It matters not how strait the gate,
How charged with punishments the scroll,
I am the master of my fate,
I am the captain of my soul.
-Henley

Henley did not write this poem until after he had discovered the door to that secret passage-way which I have mentioned.

You are the "master of your fate" and the "captain of your soul," by reason of the fact that you control your own thoughts, and, with the aid of your thoughts, you may create whatever you desire.

. . . .

As we approach the close of this lesson, let us pull aside the curtain that hangs over the gateway called death and take a look into the Great Beyond. Behold a world peopled with beings who function without the aid of physical bodies. Look closely and, whether for weal or for woe, observe that you look at a world peopled with beings of your own creation, which correspond exactly to the nature of your own thoughts as you expressed them before death. There they are, the children of your own heart and mind, patterned after the image of your own thoughts.

Those which were born of your hatred and envy and jealousy and selfishness and injustice toward your fellow men will not make very desirable neighbors, but you must live with them just the same, for they are your children and you cannot turn them out. You will be unfortunate, indeed, if you find there no children which were born of love, and justice, and truth, and kindness toward others.

In the light of this allegorical suggestion, the subject of accurate thought takes on a new and a much more important aspect, doesn't it?

If there is a possibility that every thought you release during this life will step out, in the form of aliving being, to greet you after death, then you need no further reason for guarding all your thoughts more carefully than you would guard the food that you feed your physical body.

I refer to this suggestion as "allegorical" for a reason that you will understand only after you shall have passed through the door of that secret passage-way to knowledge that I have heretofore mentioned.

To ask me how I know these things, before you pass through that door, would be as useless as it would be for a man who has never seen with his physical eyes to ask me what the color red looks like.

I am not urging you to accept this viewpoint. I am not even arguing its soundness. I am merely fulfilling my duty and discharging my responsibility by giving you the suggestion. You must carry it out to a point at which you can accept or reject it, in your own way,, and of your own volition.

The term "accurate thought" as used in this lesson refers to thought which is of your own creation. Thought that comes to you from others, through either suggestion or direct statement, is not accurate thought within the meaning and purpose of this lesson, although it may be thought that is based upon facts.

I have now carried you to the apex of the pyramid of this lesson on accurate thought. I can take you no further. However, you have not gone the entire distance; you have but started. From here on you must be your own guide, but, if you have not wholly missed the great truth upon which the lesson is founded, yarn will not have difficulty in finding your own way.

Let me caution you, however, not to become dis-courage if the fundamental truth of this lesson does not dawn upon you at first reading. It may require weeks or even months of meditation for you to comprehend fully this truth, but it is worth working for. The principles laid down in the beginning of this lesson you can easily understand and accept, because they are of the most elementary nature. However, as you began to follow the chain of thought along toward the close of the lesson, you perhaps found yourself being carried into waters too deep for you to fathom. Perhaps I can throw one final ray of light on the subject by reminding you that the sound of every voice, and of every note of music, and of every other nature that is being released at the time you are reading these lines is floating through the ether right where you are. To hear these sounds you need but the aid of a modern radio outfit. Without this equipment as a supplement to your own sense of hearing you are powerless to hear these sounds. Had this same statement been made twenty years ago, you would have believed the one who made it to be insane or a fool. But you now accept the statement without question, because you know it is true.

Thought is a much higher and more perfectly organized form of energy than is mere sound; therefore, it is not beyond the bounds of reason to suppose that every thought now being released and every thought that has ever been released is also in the ether (or somewhere else) and may be interpreted by those who have the equipment with which to do it.

And, what sort of equipment is necessary? you ask.

That will be answered when you shall have passed through the door that leads to the secret passage-way to knowledge. It cannot be answered before. The passage-way can be reached only through the medium of your own thoughts. This is one reason why all the great philosophers of the past admonished man to know himself. "Know thyself" is and has been the cry of the ages.

One of the unanswerable mysteries of God's work is the fact that this great discovery is always self-discovery. The truth for which man is eternally searching is wrapped up in his own being; therefore, it is fruitless to search far afield in the wilderness of life or in the hearts of other men to find it. To do so brings you no nearer that which you are seeking, but takes you further away from it.

And, it may be - who knows but you? - that even now, as you finish this lesson, you are nearer the door that leads to the secret passage-way to knowledge than you have ever been before.

With your mastery of this lesson will come a fuller understanding of the principle referred to in the Introductory Lesson as the "Master Mind." Surely you now understand the reason for friendly co-operative alliance between two or more people. This alliance "steps up" the minds of those who participate in it, and permits them to contact their thought-power with infinite intelligence. With this statement the entire Introductory Lesson should have a new meaning for you. This lesson has familiarized you with the main reason why you should make use of the law of the Master Mind byshowing you the height to which this law may be made to carry all who understand and use it.

By this time you should understand why a few men have risen to great heights of power and fortune, while others all around them remained in poverty and want. If you do not now understand the cause for this, you will by the time you master the remaining lessons of this course.

Do not become discouraged if complete understanding of these principles does not follow your first reading of this lesson. This is the one lesson of the entire course which cannot be fully assimilated by the beginner through one reading. It will give up its rich treasures of knowledge only through thought, reflection and meditation. For this reason you are instructed to read this lesson at least four times, at intervals of one week apart.

You are also instructed to read, again, the Introductory Lesson, that you may more accurately and definitely understand the law of the Master Mind and the relationship between this law and the subjects covered by this lesson on accurate thought.

The Master Mind is the principle through which you may become an accurate thinker!

Is not this statement both plain and significant?

FAILURE

An After-the-Lesson Visit With the Author
The Great Success Lessons That Can Be
Learned From Reverses.

AN all-wise Providence has arranged the affairs of mankind so that every person who comes into the age of reason must bear the cross of FAILURE in one form or another.

You see, in the picture at the top of this page, the heaviest and most cruel of all the crosses, POVERTY!

Hundreds of millions of people living on this earth today find it necessary to struggle under the burden of this cross in order to enjoy the three bare necessities of life, a place to sleep, something to eat and clothes to wear.

Carrying the cross of POVERTY is no joke!

But, it seems significant that the greatest and most successful men and women who ever lived found it necessary to carry this cross before they "arrived."

. . . .

FAILURE is generally accepted as a curse. But few people ever understand that failure is a curse onlywhen it is accepted as such.

But few ever learn the truth that FAILURE is seldom permanent.

Go back over your own experiences for a few years and you will see that your failures generally turned out to be blessings in disguise.

Failure teaches men lessons which they would never learn without it. Moreover, it teaches in a language that is universal. Among the great lessons taught by failure is that of HUMILITY.

No man may become great without feeling himself humble and insignificant when compared to the world about him and the stars above him and the harmony with which Nature does her work.

For every rich man's son who becomes a useful, constructive worker in behalf of humanity, there are ninety-nine others rendering useful service who come up through POVERTY and misery. This seems more than a coincidence!

. . . .

Most people who believe themselves to be failures are not failures at all. Most conditions which people look upon as failure are nothing more than temporary defeat.

If you pity yourself and feel that you are a failure, think how much worse off you would be if you had to change places with others who have real cause for complaint.

In the city of Chicago lives a beautiful young woman. Her eyes are a light blue. Her complexion is extremely fair. She has a sweet charming voice. She is educated and cultured. Three days after graduating inone of the colleges of the East she discovered that she had negro blood in her veins.

The man to whom she was engaged refused to marry her. The negroes do not want her and the whites will not associate with her. During the remainder of her life she must bear the brand of permanent FAILURE.

Remember, this is PERMANENT failure!

As this essay is being written news comes of a beautiful girl baby who was born to an unwed girl and taken into an orphanage, there to be brought up mechanically, without ever knowing the influence of a mother's love. All through life this unfortunate child must bear the brunt of another's mistake which can never be corrected.

How fortunate are YOU, no matter what may be your imaginary failures, that you are not this child.

If you have a strong body and a sound mind you have much for which you ought to be thankful. Millions of people all about you have no such blessings.

. . . .

Careful analysis of one hundred men and women whom the world has accepted as being "great" shows that they were compelled to undergo hardship and temporary defeat and failure such as YOU probably have never known and never will know.

Woodrow Wilson went to his grave altogether too soon, the victim of cruel slander and disappointment, believing, no doubt, that he was a FAILURE. TIME, the great miracle worker that rights all wrongs and turns failure into success, will place the name ofWoodrow Wilson at the top of the page of the really great.

Few now living have the vision to see that out of Wilson's "FAILURE" will come, eventually, such a powerful demand for universal peace that war will be an impossibility.

Lincoln died without knowing that his "FAILURE" gave sound foundation to the greatest nation on this earth.

Columbus died, a prisoner in chains, without ever knowing that his "FAILURE" meant the discovery of the great nation which Lincoln and Wilson helped to preserve, with their "FAILURES."

Do not use the word FAILURE carelessly.

Remember, carrying a burdensome cross temporarily is not FAILURE. If you have the real seed of success within you, a little adversity and temporary defeat will only serve to nuture that seed and cause it to burst forth into maturity.

When Divine Intelligence wants a great man or woman to render some needed service in the world, the fortunate one is tested out through some form of FAILURE. If you are undergoing what you believe to be failure, have patience; you may be passing through your testing time.

No capable executive would select, as his lieutenants, those whom he had not tested for reliability, loyalty, perseverance and other essential qualities.

Responsibility, and all that goes with it in the way of remuneration, always gravitates to the person who will not accept temporary defeat as permanent failure.

"The test of a man is the fight he makes,
The grit that he daily shows;
The way he stands on his feet and takes
Fate's numerous bumps and blows,
A coward can smile when there's naught to fear,
When nothing his progress bars;
But it takes a man to stand up and cheer
While some other fellow stars.

"It isn't the victory, after all,
But the fight that a brother makes;
The man who, driven against the wall,
Still stands up erect and takes
The blows of fate with his head held high:
Bleeding, and bruised, and pale,

Is the man who'll win in the by and by,
For he isn't afraid to fail.

"It's the bumps you get, and the jolts you get,
And the shocks that your courage stands,
The hours of sorrow and vain regret,
The prize that escapes your hands,
That test your mettle and prove your worth;
It isn't the blows you deal,
But the blows you take on the good old earth,
That show if your stuff is real."

Failure often places one in a position where unusual effort must be forthcoming. Many a man has wrung victory from defeat, fighting with his back to the wall, where he could not retreat.

Caesar had long wished to conquer the British. He quietly sailed his soldier-laden ships to the British island, unloaded his troops and supplies, then gave the order to burn all the ships. Calling his soldiers about him he said: "Now it is win or perish. We have no choice."

They won! Men usually win when they make up their minds to do so.

Burn your bridges behind you and observe how well you work when you KNOW THAT YOU HAVE NO RETREAT.

A street car conductor got a leave of absence while he tried out a position in a great mercantile business. "If I do not succeed in holding my new position," he remarked to a friend, "I can always come back to the old job."

At the end of the month he was back, completely cured of all ambition to do anything except work on a street car. Had he resigned instead of asking for a leave of absence he might have made good in the new job.

· · · · · · · ·

The Thirteen Club movement, which is now spreading over the entire country, was born as the result of a shocking disappointment experienced by its founder. That shock was sufficient to open the mind to a broader and more comprehensive view of the needs of the age, and this discovery led to the creation of one of the most outstanding influences of this generation.

The Fifteen Laws of Success, upon which this course is based, grew out of twenty years of hardship and poverty and failure such as rarely come to one person in an entire lifetime.

Surely those of you who have followed this series of lessons from the beginning must have read between the lines and back of them a story of struggle which has meant self-discipline and self-discovery such asnever would have been known without this hardship.

. . . .

Study the roadway of life, in the picture at the beginning of this essay, and observe that everyone who travels that road carries a cross. Remember, as you take inventory of your own burdens, that Nature's richest gifts go to those who meet FAILURE without flinching or whining.

Nature's ways are not easily understood. If they were, no one could be tested for great responsibility, with FAILURE!

"When Nature wants to make a man,
And shake a man,
And wake a man;
When Nature wants to make a man
To do the Future's will;
When she tries with all her skill
And she yearns with all her soul
To create him large and whole...
With what cunning she prepares him!
How she goads and never spares him!
How she whets him, and she frets him,
And in poverty begets him....
How she often disappoints
How she often anoints,
With what wisdom she will hide him,
Never minding what betide him
Though his genius sob with slighting
And his pride may not forget!
Bids him struggle harder yet.
Makes him lonely
So that only
God's high messages shall reach him,
So that she may surely teach him
What the Hierarchy planned.

Though he may not understand
Gives him passions to command.
How remorselessly she spurs him
With terrific ardor stirs him
When she poignantly prefers him!

* * *

Lo, the crisis! Lo, the shout
That must call the leader out.
When the people need salvation
Doth he come to lead the nation....
Then doth Nature show her plan
When the world has found - A MAN!"

There is no FAILURE. That which looks to be failure is usually
nothing but temporary defeat. Make sure that you do not accept it
as PERMANENT!

BN Publishing
We have Book Recommendations for you

Automatic Wealth: The Secrets of the Millionaire Mind--Including: Acres of Diamonds, As a Man Thinketh, I Dare you!, The Science of Getting Rich, The Way to Wealth, and Think and Grow Rich
by Napoleon Hill, et al

Think and Grow Rich [MP3 AUDIO] [UNABRIDGED]
by Napoleon Hill, Jason McCoy (Narrator)

As a Man Thinketh [UNABRIDGED]
by James Allen, Jason McCoy (Narrator)

Your Invisible Power: How to Attain Your Desires by Letting Your Subconscious Mind Work for You [MP3 AUDIO] [UNABRIDGED]
by Genevieve Behrend, Jason McCoy (Narrator)

Thought Vibration or the Law of Attraction in the Thought World [MP3 AUDIO] [UNABRIDGED]
by William Walker Atkinson, Jason McCoy (Narrator)

Breinigsville, PA USA
12 April 2010
235992BV00001B/109/A